The *Focus on the Family* ®

Guide to

Growing a Healthy Marriage

The *Focus on the Family* ®

Guide to

Growing a
Healthy
Marriage

PUBLISHING

Colorado Springs, Colorado

GROWING A HEALTHY MARRIAGE

Copyright © 1993 by Focus on the Family. All Rights Reserved. International Copyright Secured.

ISBN 1-56179-210-1

Published by Focus on the Family Publishing, Colorado Springs, CO 80995. United States of America.

Designer: Multnomah Graphics
Editor: Mike Yorkey

Printed in the United States of America

93 94 95 96 97 98 / 10 9 8 7 6 5 4 3 2 1

CONTENTS

FOREWORD

O ne of the most challenging and sobering tasks that I do each week is to read the letters that come into CARE for the Family. That correspondence is so varied as a husband, wife or perhaps a teenager asks for counsel in the situation that is being experienced in their family. What is common to all is a cry for materials—books, videos, tapes—that will help. The main requirement seems to be that such resources are practical and down to earth.

The Focus on the Family Guide to Growing a Healthy Marriage is such a book. *Focus on the Family* magazine is read by millions each month and here is the very best of it in one volume - 37 articles in five handy categories. I confess that as my wife Dianne and I scanned the contents page, we glanced at each other and vowed to do some serious reading! There is no marriage on the face of the earth that can do without ongoing help and encouragement. We are foolish if we expect to avoid all the tough times.

For those who are not familiar with Focus on the Family, it is an American charitable organization founded by Dr. James Dobson, a psychologist and author of 13 best selling books on family issues. There is nobody in the whole family arena that I respect more highly.

This is a book destined to become dog-eared through much use. Buy a copy as a gift for a friend or a couple about to be married, but don't give yours away! This is a resource to pick up again and again. I hope you enjoy it.

—Rob Parsons
Executive Director
CARE for the Family

PART ONE

FOCUS ON MARRIAGE

❦ 1

Prescription for a Successful Marriage

Dr. James C. Dobson

*I*n an effort to draw on the experiences of those who have lived together successfully as husbands and wives, we asked married couples to participate in an informal study. More than 600 people agreed to speak candidly to the younger generation about the concepts and methods that have worked in their homes. They each wrote comments and recommendations which were carefully analyzed and compared.

The advice they offered is not new, but it certainly represents a great place to begin. In attempting to learn any task, one should start with the *fundamentals*—those initial steps from which everything else will later develop. In this spirit, our panel of 600 offered three tried-

and-tested, back-to-basic recommendations with which no committed Christian would likely disagree.

Christ-Centered Home

The panel first suggests that newlyweds should establish and maintain a *Christ-centered home.* Everything rests on that foundation. If a young husband and wife are deeply committed to Jesus Christ, they enjoy enormous advantages over the family with no spiritual dimension.

A meaningful prayer life is essential in maintaining a Christ-centered home. Of course, some people use prayer the way they follow their horoscopes, attempting to manipulate an unidentified "higher power" around them. One of my friends teasingly admits that he utters a prayer each morning on the way to work when he passes the donut shop. He knows it is unhealthy to eat the greasy pastries, but he loves them dearly. Therefore, he asks the Lord for permission to indulge himself each day.

He'll say, "If it is Your will that I have a donut this morning, let there be a parking space available somewhere as I circle the block." If no spot can be found for his car, he circles the block and prays again.

Shirley and I have taken our prayer life a bit more seriously. In fact, this communication between us and God has been the stabilizing factor throughout our 33 years of married life. In good times, in hard times, in moments of anxiety and in periods of praise, we have shared this wonderful privilege of talking directly to our Heavenly Father. What a concept! No appointment is needed to enter into His presence. We don't have to go through His subordinates or bribe His secretaries. He is simply there, whenever we bow before Him. Some of the highlights of my life have occurred in these quiet sessions with the Lord.

I'll never forget the time when our daughter had just learned to drive. Danae had been enrolled in Kamakazi Driving School, and the moment finally arrived for her to take her first solo flight in the family car. Believe me, my anxiety level was climbing off the chart that day.

Someday you will know how terrifying it is to hand the car keys to a 16-year-old kid who doesn't know what she doesn't know about driving. Shirley and I stood quaking in the front yard as Danae drove out of sight. We then turned to go back into the house, and I said, "Well, Babe, the Lord giveth and the Lord taketh away."

Fortunately, Danae made it home safely in a few minutes and brought the car to a careful and controlled stop. That is the sweetest sound in the world to an anxious parent!

It was during this era, when we lived in Southern California, that Shirley and I covenanted between us to pray for our son and daughter at the close of every day. Not only were we concerned about the risk of an automobile accident, but we were also aware of so many other dangers that lurk out there in a city like Los Angeles.

That part of the world is known for weirdos, kooks, nuts, ding-a-lings, and fruitcakes. That's one reason we found ourselves on our knees each evening, asking for divine protection for the teenagers we love so much.

One night we were particularly tired and collapsed into bed without our benedictory prayer. We were almost asleep before Shirley's voice pierced the night. "Jim," she said. "We haven't prayed for our kids yet today. Don't you think we should talk to the Lord?"

I admit it was difficult for me to pull my 6'2" frame out of the warm bed that night. Nevertheless, we got on our knees and offered a prayer for our children's safety, placing them in the hands of the Father once more.

Later we learned that Danae and a girlfriend had gone to a fast-food establishment and bought hamburgers and Cokes. They drove up the road a few miles to eat the meal when a city policeman drove by, shining his spotlight in all directions. He was obviously looking for someone, but gradually went past.

In a few minutes, Danae and her friend heard a "clunk" from under the car. They looked at one another nervously and felt another sharp bump. Before they could leave, a man crawled out from under the car and emerged on the passenger side. He was very hairy and looked as if he had been on the street for weeks. He also wore strange-looking "John Lennon" glasses down on his nose. The man immediately came over to the door and attempted to open it. Thank God, it was locked. Danae quickly started the car and drove off . . . no doubt at record speed.

Later, when we checked the timing of this incident, we realized that Shirley and I had been on our knees at the precise moment of danger. Our prayers were answered. Our daughter and her friend were safe!

It is impossible for me to overstate the need for prayer in the fabric of family life. Not simply as a shield against danger, of course. A personal relationship with Jesus Christ is the cornerstone of marriage, giving meaning and purpose to every dimension of living. Being able to bow in prayer as the day begins or ends gives expression to the frustrations and concerns that might not otherwise be ventilated.

On the other end of that prayer line is a loving Heavenly Father who has promised to hear and answer our petitions. In this day of disintegrating families on every side, we dare not try to make it on our own.

Commitment

I attended the 50th wedding anniversary for two friends a few years ago, and the man made an incredible statement to his guests. He said he and his wife had never had a serious fight or argument in the 50 years since they were married. That was either a lot of baloney or he and his wife had a very boring relationship. Maybe both were true.

To newly married couples I must say: Don't count on having that kind of placid relationship. There will be times of conflict and disagreement. There will be periods of emotional blandness when you can generate nothing but a yawn for one another. That's life, as they say.

What will you do, then, when unexpected tornadoes blow through your home, or when the doldrums leave your sails sagging and silent? Will you pack it in and go home to Mama? Will you pout and cry and seek ways to strike back? Or will your commitment hold you steady?

These questions must be addressed *now*, before Satan has an opportunity to put his noose of discouragement around your neck. Set your jaw and clench your fists. Nothing short of death must ever be permitted to come between the two of you. *Nothing!*

This determined attitude is missing from so many marital relationships today. I read of a wedding ceremony in New York a few years ago where the bride and groom each pledged "to stay with you for as long as I shall love you." I doubt if their marriage lasted even to this time.

The feeling of love is simply too ephemeral to hold a relationship together for very long. It comes and goes. That's why our panel of 600 was adamant at this point. They have lived long enough to know that a weak marital commitment will inevitably end in divorce.

Communication

Another recommendation by our panel represents a basic ingredient for a good marriage—good communication between husbands and wives. This topic has been beaten to death by writers of books on the subject of marriage, so I will hit it lightly. I would like to offer a few less overworked thoughts on marital communication, however, that might be useful to young married couples.

First, it must be understood that males and females differ in yet another way not mentioned earlier. Research makes it clear that little girls are blessed with greater linguistic ability than little boys, and it remains a lifelong talent. Simply stated, she talks more than he.

As an adult, she typically expresses her feelings and thoughts far better than her husband and is often irritated by his reticence. God may have given her 50,000 words per day and her husband only 25,000. He comes home with 24,975 used up and merely grunts his way through the evening. He may descend into "Monday Night Football" while his wife is dying to expend her remaining 25,000 words.

Erma Bombeck complained about this tendency of men to get lost in televised sports while their wives hunger for companionship. She even proposed that a new ordinance be passed that would be called "Bombeck's Law." According to it, a man who had watched 168,000 football games in a single season could be declared legally dead. All in favor say "Aye."

The complexity of the human personality guarantees exceptions to every generalization. Yet women do tend to talk more than men. Every knowledgeable marriage counselor knows that the inability or unwillingness of husbands to reveal their feelings to their wives is one of the common complaints of women.

It can almost be stated as an absolute: Show me a quiet, reserved husband, and I'll show you a frustrated wife. She wants to know what he's thinking and what happened at his office and how he sees the children and, especially, how he feels about her. The husband, by contrast, finds some things better left unsaid. It is a classic struggle.

The paradox is that a highly emotional, verbal woman is sometimes drawn to the strong, silent type. He seemed so secure and "in control" before they were married. She admired his unflappable nature and his coolness in a crisis.

Then they were married, and the flip side of his great strength became obvious. He wouldn't talk! She then gnashed her teeth for the next 40 years because her husband couldn't give what she needed from him. It just wasn't in him.

Lyricist and singer Paul Simon wrote a song entitled "I Am a Rock," which expressed the sentiment of a silent introvert. The person about whom the song is written has been wounded and has pulled within himself for protection. As you read these lyrics, imagine the special communication problems such a man and his poor wife would experience in marriage.

> A winter's day
>
> In a deep and dark December
> I am alone,
> Gazing from my window
> To the streets below
> On a freshly fallen silent shroud of snow.
>
> I am a rock.
> I am an island.
>
> I've built walls,
> A fortress deep and mighty,
> That none may penetrate.
> I have no need of friendship
> Friendship causes pain.
> Its laughter and its loving I disdain.
>
> I am a rock.
> I am an island.
>
> Don't talk of love;
> Well I've heard the word before;
> It's sleeping in my memory.
> I won't disturb the slumber of feelings that have died.
> If I never loved I never would have cried.

I am a rock.
I am an island.

I have my books
And my poetry to protect me;
I am shielded in my armour,
Hiding in my room,
Safe within my womb.
I touch no one and no one touches me.

I am a rock.
I am an island.

And a rock feels no pain;
And an island never cries.

Unfortunately, the wives and children of rocks and islands do feel pain, and they *do* cry! But what is the solution to such communicative problems at home? As always, it involves compromise. A man has a clear responsibility to "cheer up his wife which he has taken" (Deuteronomy 24:5). He must not claim himself "a rock" who will never allow himself to be vulnerable again. He must press himself to open his heart and share his deeper feelings with his wife.

Time must be reserved for meaningful conversations. Taking walks and going out to breakfast and riding bicycles on Saturday mornings are conversation inducers that keep love alive. Communication can occur even in families where the husband leans inward and the wife leans outward. In these instances, I believe, the primary responsibility for compromise lies with the husband.

On the other hand, women must understand and accept the fact that some men cannot be what they want them to be. I have previously addressed this need for wives to accept reality as it is presented to them in *What Wives Wish Their Husbands Knew About Women.*

Can you accept the fact that your husband will never be able to meet all your needs and aspirations? Seldom does one human being satisfy every longing and hope in the breast of another.

Obviously, this coin has two sides: You can't be his perfect woman, either. He is no more equipped to resolve your entire package of emotional needs than you are to become his sexual dream machine every 24 hours. Both partners have to settle for human foibles and faults and irritability and fatigue and occasional nighttime "headaches."

A good marriage is not one where perfection reigns: It is a relationship where a healthy perspective overlooks a multitude of "unresolvables." Thank goodness my wife, Shirley, has adopted this attitude toward me!

I am especially concerned about the mother of small children who chooses to stay at home as a full-time homemaker. If she looks to her husband as a provider of all adult conversation and the satisfier of every emotional need, their marriage can quickly run aground. He will return home from work somewhat depleted and in need of "tranquility," as we discussed earlier.

Instead, he finds a woman who is continually starved for attention and support. When she sees in his eyes that he has nothing left to give, that is the beginning of sorrows. She either becomes depressed or angry (or both), and he has no idea how he can help her. I understand this feminine need and have attempted to articulate it to men.

Nevertheless, a woman's total dependence on a man places too great a pressure on the marital relationship. It sometimes cracks under the strain.

What can be done, then? A woman with a normal range of emotional needs cannot simply ignore them. They scream for fulfillment. Consequently, I have long recommended that women in this situation seek to supplement what their husbands can give by cultivating meaningful female relationships.

Having girlfriends with whom they can talk heart-to-heart, study the Scriptures, and share child-care techniques can be vital to mental health. Without this additional support, loneliness and low self-esteem can accumulate and begin to choke the marriage to death.

This solution of feminine company seems so obvious that one might ask why it is even worthwhile to suggest it. Unfortunately, it is not so easy to implement. A woman must often search for companionship today. We've witnessed a breakdown in relationships between women in recent years.

A hundred years ago, wives and mothers did not have to seek

female friendship. It was programmed into the culture. Women canned food together, washed clothes at the creek together, and cooperated in church charity work together.

When babies were born, the new mother was visited by aunts, sisters, neighbors, and church women who came to help her diaper, feed, and care for the child. There was an automatic support system that surrounded women and made life easier. Its absence translates quickly into marital conflict and can lead to divorce.

To the young wives who are reading these words, I urge you *not to let this scenario happen to you*. Invest some time in your female friends—even though you are busy. Resist the temptation to pull into the walls of your home and wait for your husband to be all things to you. Stay involved as a family in a church that meets your needs and preaches the Word.

Remember that you are surrounded by many other women with similar feelings. Find them. Care for them. Give to them. And in the process, your own self-esteem will rise. Then when you are content, your marriage will flourish.

It sounds simplistic, but that's the way we are made. We are designed to love God and to love one another. Deprivation of either function can be devastating.

Dr. Dobson now lives in Colorado Springs, where Focus on the Family is headquartered. Excerpted from *Love for a Lifetime*, ©1987 by James C. Dobson. Published by Questar Publishers. Used by permission.

2

"Why Can't My Spouse Understand What I Say?"

Gary Smalley and John Trent, Ph.D.

A number of years ago, I (Gary) sat down to talk with an attractive woman who was in obvious pain. With tears streaming down her face, she sobbed, "I've tried to express what's wrong in our marriage, but I just can't seem to explain it. What's the use in bringing it all up again?"

After only five years of marriage, this woman had nearly given up hope of experiencing a loving, healthy, and lasting relationship with her husband. Opposed to divorce, she had resigned herself to a life that offered few of the wishes and dreams for which she longed.

13

I had heard this kind of story before. For years, I had regularly counseled with husbands and wives, spending countless hours talking to them about improving their relationships. Only now, I wasn't sitting in my counseling office. I was seated at my kitchen table. And the woman sitting across from me wasn't a counselee—she was my own wife, Norma!

That day, I made a decision to understand what was happening, or not happening, in my marriage. And I also decided to find the answers to several important questions. Why was Norma feeling so frustrated in her attempts to communicate with me? Why did I have such a difficult time sharing my feelings with her? And why was it such a struggle to understand each other—particularly when we discussed important issues?

While I didn't realize it at the time, the answer to these questions was, in large part, all in our minds. It wasn't until we understood why males and females think and speak so differently that we began maximizing our communication. The bridge that spanned these differences proved to be "emotional word pictures."

Unlike anything we have seen, word pictures can supercharge communication and change lives, whether in marriages, families, friendships, or businesses. Indeed, word pictures have the capacity to capture people's attention by engaging both their thoughts and their feelings.

Have you ever tried to express an important thought or feeling to members of the opposite sex, only to have them act as if you're speaking a foreign language? Have you ever asked, "Why can't he (or she) *feel* what I'm saying?" Join the club.

Throughout history, many women have found it difficult (some say impossible!) to communicate with men. And an equal number of men have given up trying to converse with women. I ran into this problem myself on a shopping trip when my wife and I were using the same words, but speaking a different language.

"Shoooopppping"

After that tearful session with my wife, I decided to commit myself wholeheartedly to understanding and relating to her. But I didn't know where to start.

Suddenly, I had an idea I knew would get me nominated for Husband of the Year. I could do something adventurous with Norma—

like going shopping!

I'm not sure what emotional and physiological changes ignite inside my wife upon hearing the words *the mall*, but when I told her my idea, it was obvious something dramatic was happening. Her eyes lit up like a Christmas tree, and she trembled with excitement—the same reaction I'd had when someone gave me two tickets to an NFL playoff game.

That next Saturday afternoon, as we drove up to the mall, Norma told me she needed to look for a new blouse. So after we parked the car and walked into the nearest clothing store, she held up a blouse and asked, "What do you think?"

"Great," I said. "Let's get it." But really, I was thinking, *Great! If she hurries up and gets this blouse, we'll be back home in plenty of time to watch the college game on TV.*

Then she picked up another blouse and said, "What do you think about this one?"

"It's great, too!" I said. "Get either one. No, get both!"

But after looking at a number of blouses on the rack, we walked out of the store empty-handed. Then we went into another store, and she did the same thing. And then into another store. And another. And another!

As we went in and out of all the shops, I became increasingly anxious. The thought even struck me, *Not only will I miss the half-time highlights, but at the rate we're going, I will miss the entire season!* And that's when it happened.

Instead of picking up a blouse at the next store we entered, she held up a dress that was our daughter's size. "What do you think about this for Kari?" she asked.

Taxed beyond any mortal's limits, my willpower cracked, and I blurted out, "What do you mean, 'What do I think about a dress for Kari?' We're here shopping for blouses for you, not dresses for Kari!"

That night, I began to understand a common difference between men and women. I wasn't shopping for blouses . . . I was *hunting* for blouses! I wanted to conquer the blouse, bag it, and then get back home where important things waited—like my Saturday afternoon football game!

My wife, however, looked at shopping from the opposite extreme. For her, it meant more than simply buying a blouse. It was a way to spend time talking together as we enjoyed several hours away from the children—and Saturday afternoon football.

Like most men, I thought a trip to the mall meant going shopping. But to my wife, it meant shooooppping!

Over the next several days, I thought back to our mall experience and my commitment to become a better communicator. As I reflected on our afternoon, I realized I had overlooked something important— the innate differences between men and women.

Gaining the Edge in Communication

Researchers have found that from the earliest years, little girls talk more than little boys. One study showed that even in the hospital nursery, girls have more lip movement than boys! That propensity keeps right on increasing through the years, giving them an edge at meaningful communication!

In our home, Norma noticed the same thing discovered by Harvard's Preschool Program in its research of communication differences between the sexes. After wiring a playground for sounds, researchers found that 100 percent of the sounds coming from the girls' mouths were audible, recognizable words.

As for the little boys, only 68 percent of their sounds were understandable words! The remaining 32 percent were either one-syllable sounds like "uh" and "mmm" or sound effects like "Varooom!" "Yaaaaah!" and "Zooooom!"

Norma was comforted to discover that the propensity males had in our family to yell and grunt was caused by heredity, not environment. And after 20-plus years of asking me questions and receiving monosyllabic answers like "uh" and "mmm," she claims this inability to communicate in understandable sentences remains constant throughout the male life span!

Are Men Really Brain Damaged?

From the Garden of Eden, when Eve needed more fig leaves than Adam, it's been clear that men and women differ physically. However, only recently has research shown that they have uniquely different thought patterns.

Specifically, medical studies have shown that between the 18th and 26th week of pregnancy, something happens that forever separates the sexes. Using heat-sensitive color monitors, researchers have actually observed a chemical bath of testosterone and other sex-related hormones wash over a baby boy's brain. This causes changes that never happen to the brain of a baby girl. Here's a layman's explanation of what happens when those chemicals hit a boy's system:

The human brain is divided into two halves, or hemispheres, connected by fibrous tissue called the *corpus callosum*. The sex-related hormones and chemicals that flood a baby boy's brain cause the right side to recede slightly, destroying some of the connecting fibers. One result is that, in most cases, a boy starts life more *left*-brain oriented.

Because little girls don't experience this chemical bath, they leave the starting blocks much more two-sided in their thinking. And while electrical impulses and messages do travel back and forth between both sides of a baby boy's brain, those same messages can proceed faster and be less hindered in the brain of a little girl.

Now wait a minute, you may be thinking. *Does this mean that men are basically brain damaged?*

Well, not exactly. What occurs in the womb merely sets the stage for men and women to "specialize" in two different ways of thinking. And this is one major reason men and women need each other so much.

The left brain houses more of the logical, analytical, factual, and aggressive centers of thought. It's the side of the brain most men reserve for the majority of their waking hours. It enjoys conquering 500 miles a day on family vacation trips; favors mathematical formulas over romance novels; stores the dictionary definition of love; and generally favors clinical, black-and-white thinking.

On the other hand, most women spend the majority of their days and nights camped out on the right side of the brain. It's the side that harbors the center for feelings, as well as the primary relational language and communication skills; enables them to do fine-detail work; sparks imagination; and makes an afternoon devoted to art and fine music actually enjoyable. Perhaps you now can begin to understand why communication is difficult in marriage.

However, there is a way for a man to boost his communication skills instantly and for a woman to multiply hers. By using the power of emotional word pictures to open his right brain, a man can move beyond "facts" and begin to achieve total communication with a woman. This same skill not only will help a woman get a man to *feel* her words as well as *hear* them, but it also will maximize her innate relational abilities.

Years ago, Norma proved this point to me. She illustrated a concern in such a way that her words immediately moved from my head to my heart.

Add Feelings to Facts

When I was working on my parenting book, *The Key to Your Child's Heart*, I asked Norma if she would write one of the chapters. It was a section that highlighted one of her strengths, and I thought the project would be an easy and pleasurable experience for her. I thought wrong.

As the days passed and time drew near for the chapter to be completed, Norma hadn't even started. Several times she tried to discuss how much of a burden the project was, but I always steered the conversation back to the "facts."

I decided it was time to motivate her. I told her that writing a book was absolutely no big deal. She wrote excellent letters, I pointed out. She ought to think of the chapter as just one long letter to thousands of people she'd never met. What's more, I assured her, as a seasoned publishing veteran, I would personally critique each and every page and catch her slightest error. I thought to myself, *Is this motivation, or what?*

Her emotional, right-brain appeals to duck the assignment made little impact on me, because I was armed with the facts. But my left-brain reasoning didn't impress her much, either. We traded words as if we were swapping Monopoly money. Frankly, we should have saved our breath. We were at loggerheads until my wife, in desperation, gave me the following word picture.

"Do you see those hills in the distance?" she asked, pointing out the window. "Every day I feel like I must climb them, wearing a 20-pound backpack. Between getting the kids fed, dressed, to school, and to their athletic practices—and still managing our business office—I barely have enough energy to take another step.

"Now, don't get me wrong," she continued. "I work out to stay in shape, and I love walking those hills daily. But you're doing something that's like asking me to climb Squaw Peak every day—in addition to climbing those hills."

"I am?" I said, pondering her words. Several months earlier I had climbed Squaw Peak, a beautiful mountain near our home, and I knew firsthand how demanding its incline was. My mind shifted into the hypersearch mode to determine where Norma was headed with the story. "Okay, I'm stumped," I finally said. "What in the world am I doing to force Squaw Peak on you?"

"You added Squaw Peak to my day when you asked me to write that chapter for the book. For you, carrying around a 20-pound pack is nothing. But to me, the weight of my current responsibilities takes all my energy. Honey, I just can't add another pound, climb the hills, and take on Squaw Peak as well."

Suddenly, everything she had been saying before was clear. To me, writing a chapter wouldn't have added an extra ounce to my pack or caused the slightest additional incline to the hills I climb daily. But for the first time, I could feel the strain I'd unknowingly put her under.

"If that's what writing a chapter is like, then I wouldn't want you to do it," I said without a moment's hesitation. "I appreciate what you're already doing and don't want to weigh you down any more. You're far too valuable for that."

After the conversation, it was as if a cloud lifted from our relationship. But I didn't know what to make of things the next morning when I came down the hall for breakfast. Norma was sitting at her kitchen desk, furiously writing away.

"What are you doing?" I asked, dumbfounded.

"Writing my chapter."

"You're doing what? I thought you said it was like climbing Squaw Peak!"

"It was," she said. "When I knew I had to write it, I felt tremendous pressure. But now that I don't have to, the pressure is gone!"

Bridging the Communication Gap

No one says word pictures will help you understand all the differences between men and women. But they do help us bridge the natural communication gap—and better understand what another person is saying.

As mentioned earlier, there are two primary ways we process and remember information. The first is via the left side of the brain. It is the channel through which the literal words and factual data of conversation are stored. Since men are primarily left-brain oriented, they generally focus on the actual words being said and often miss the underlying emotions.

That's exactly what happened when Norma first discussed not writing the chapter. Her words only registered through my left brain. Consequently, they had little effect. But when she used a word picture, it was as if she began talking in color instead of black and white. I immediately saw the colors and shades of her feelings, and as a result, both my attitudes and actions changed.

If a woman truly expects to have meaningful communication with her husband, she *must* activate the right side of his brain. And if a man truly wants to communicate with his wife, he *must* enter her world of emotions. In both these regards, word pictures can serve as a tremendous aid.

Indeed, a world of colorful communication waits for those who learn the skill of bridging both sides of the brain. Word pictures won't eliminate all the differences between men and women, but they can enable us to unlock the gateway to intimacy.

Gary Smalley and John Trent are well-known authors and speakers. Excerpted from *The Language of Love*, ©1988 by Gary Smalley and John Trent, Ph.D. Published by Focus on the Family.

3

Working Through Marital Conflict

Richard and Mary Strauss

*I*t wasn't a happy evening. From the moment I walked through the door, I knew that Mary was in an irritable mood. I didn't know whether the kids had gotten to her, some church member said something unkind, or if she just wasn't feeling well. But I suspected sooner or later she might turn her wrath on me. Besides, I hadn't had a particularly pleasant day myself, and I wasn't about to look for trouble by probing for the problem.

When we had finished eating and cleaning up the kitchen, I sat down to read the newspaper. That's when it started.

"You're not going to read that paper, are you?"

"Well, yes. Why shouldn't I?"

"If you have time to read the paper, then you have time to bathe the kids and put them to bed."

"Mary, I've had a tough day, and I have to leave for a board meeting in 45 minutes. Let me relax for a while."

Though I had suspected this would happen, I still wasn't ready for it. I could feel myself getting defensive, and my response was less than understanding. We argued until I left for the meeting. When I returned home, the atmosphere was sullen and silent.

Now we were lying in bed, six inches apart, yet hundreds of miles from each other emotionally, both bodies as stiff as Egyptian mummies. Neither one dared to move an arm or leg lest it accidentally touch the other and be interpreted as a desire to talk it out, or—horror of horrors—apologize! We were in for another long night of conflict.

Bumpy Roads to Resolution

Of course, there are as many ways to react to conflict as there are personality types.

Some people simply withdraw. They think the best way to solve a problem is to run from it. But that doesn't solve anything. It just builds a wall between them, as I can sadly testify.

Other people fight to win. They won't quit until they've proved that they're right and their opponent is wrong. But that just drives their mates further away from them, as Mary can unhappily attest.

A third response is to yield. The person who always yields may think he is right, but it's not worth the hassle to prove it, so he just gives in and tries to forget the whole thing. But that builds resentment, which is sure to come out in one way or another.

A fourth method is to compromise—each one must give a little and try to meet in the middle. Sometimes that is the only way, but it does carry with it the danger that neither mate will feel completely understood or that his or her needs have been met.

A Better Way: Love Fights

Must there be conflict in marriage? Can't two reasonably intelligent and mature adults live together in peace?

Yes, they can. There will always be differences of opinion; no two normal people will always agree on everything. But they can work through those inevitable disagreements and resolve their conflicts.

How?

The best way to resolve conflict is to seek a solution that will satisfy the needs of both. Here are several things Mary and I try to do as we work toward that desirable goal. We strive to turn our conflicts into *love fights*—exchanges that not only resolve the conflict, but actually *increase* our love for one another.

The following are six principles to follow in the process of a love fight:

Adopt a learner's posture. Both spouses will win if they can learn and grow through the experience. Couples need to establish this goal from the very beginning.

Once Mary and I realize there is tension between us, the most important thing is not to make the other person understand our point of view—not to win the argument. Instead, the important thing is to learn something valuable that will help us become the person God wants us to be.

If I really want to resolve a conflict, I need to reach out and begin to work toward strengthening our relationship—even if that means being vulnerable and making some changes in *my* life.

Since neither one of us has the natural inclination to do that, it will also help to pray: "Lord, help me to have a teachable spirit. Relieve me of my defensiveness, self-righteousness, and anger, and help me learn something that will cause me to grow." If we can maintain that attitude, we're well on the way to resolving conflict.

Listen with your hearts. My normal response is to show Mary how unreasonable she is acting, correct her inaccuracies, refute her logic, pick at details, and explain why I spoke and acted as I did. But an inspired proverb says, "He whose ear listens to the life-giving reproof will dwell among the wise" (Proverbs 15:31).

We reach the root of the problem more readily if I invite her to tell me what she is feeling and what her needs are. I also ask her how she would have liked me to respond and what I can do to help resolve the problem in a way that is best for her.

My hope is that she can share her thoughts with me without hurting me. But whatever she says, my goal should be to listen—without arguing, without answering back, without justifying my actions, without trying to get her to acknowledge my needs. My only comments at this point should be to agree or to seek further clarification.

If something sounds untrue or unfair, I should simply say, "What I hear you saying is . . ." and then state my impression of what she said and ask if I'm understanding her correctly. After that, I must devote myself to listening.

Mary explains it from her vantage point:

"There are two things I would like from Richard—one is unconditional love, and the second is understanding. I want him to understand not only the meaning of the words I am saying, but what I really mean—the hidden meaning. I want him to try to feel with me—I want to feel his support even when he does not agree with me. I want to be considered valuable to him.

"But if I want him to understand me, I have to make myself understandable. I must be willing to answer questions, to share my mind honestly, to avoid becoming defensive, to make myself vulnerable, and to listen and think before I speak. And I must be willing to look at things from his viewpoint."

Keep your emotions under control. When we are falsely accused or misjudged, most of us get angry on the inside and reflect that anger in some way. Of course, our spouses can feel our displeasure.

Anger will never help us to resolve a conflict or help us grow: ". . . for the anger of a man does not achieve the righteousness of God" (James 1:20). Ephesians 4:31 says that God wants us to put our anger away from us.

How do we overcome anger? *Not* by bottling it up. If we do that, it inevitably surfaces in one form or another. Nor should we direct the anger toward ourselves—that is one of the major causes of depression.

The healthiest way to dispel anger is to admit it audibly ("I'm feeling angry right now"); identify the reason for the anger ("I feel angry when you speak sharply to me like that"); forgive the other person for failing to meet our expectations; and finally, kindly express our needs and desires to our mate. If we can do this, a resolution is just around the corner.

Think before you speak. Some of us have our mouths in motion before our minds are in gear. And if we are trying to resolve a difference, that is like pouring gasoline on a brush fire. Thinking before we speak will help us tell our mates what we are feeling and what we want—without hurting them.

Focus on your own part of the blame. Blaming others usually stems from a low self-image; we feel that we must win in order to establish our worth. Sometimes we blame others simply to avoid admitting that we have contributed to the problem.

If we are serious about strengthening a relationship, we must ask ourselves what *we* have done to agitate the conflict. If our partner feels hurt, unappreciated, criticized, or rejected, then we must examine our own attitudes, words, and actions. What have we done to contribute to those feelings? Even if our actions were unintentional, the tone of our voice or the expression on our face may have fueled the feelings, and we must be willing to acknowledge that.

Only recently have I begun to realize the ways in which I contributed to the arguments in my marriage, if by nothing more than a disapproving glance or a probing question that subtly belittles Mary. Her hostile attacks used to send me scurrying to my study, where I would sulk and pity myself for long periods of time.

Once in a great while she still comes at me rather aggressively, and my first reaction is still to run to the safety of my study. But I no sooner close the door than the Lord begins to deal with me. I don't hear any voices, but the thoughts are surely there: "What are you doing in here?"

"I just came in here to get away from the verbal barrage, Lord."

"You need to go out there and admit your part of the blame."

"But Lord, You heard what she said to me. That was totally unreasonable and untrue. It hurt. I need time to heal."

"Go out and admit your part of the blame."

Keep short accounts. It doesn't take several days for Mary and me to confront the problem anymore—usually just several minutes. And by that time, Mary has started to think about her part of the blame as well. These days, we are more readily able to acknowledge our wrong, seek the other's forgiveness, embrace, and proceed joyfully.

As the years have progressed, my work in ministry has required more traveling—good-byes are an increasing part of our relationship. There have been times when we parted without resolving a conflict, and my thought has been, *What if this were our last goodbye?*

Suppose something happened to one of us before we were reunited. Could the other live with himself/herself? It would be extremely difficult. It is our desire to keep short accounts with each other and to resolve our conflicts quickly and completely in a manner that keeps our love for one another growing stronger.

"What Are You Thinking?"

If we were to choose the one area that has caused us more problems than any other—and continues to be our weakest link—it would be the area of communication. And in that we are not alone. Many other couples echo the same frustration over their desire to communicate more effectively.

My problem was simply that I *didn't!* I've always been a rather quiet person, not prone to revealing my thoughts. Mary would ask, "What are you thinking?"

I would answer, "Oh, nothing important."

In some instances, I was ashamed to admit what I was thinking. It may have been a doubt or a fear that I didn't want to admit because I thought it would make me look weak. It may have been a wild aspiration that I didn't want to disclose because I thought she would criticize the idea, or it may have been a lustful thought that I didn't want to acknowledge for fear of being seen as spiritually lacking.

It was safer to play the role of the silent martyr. And besides, I thought that would make her suffer some for hurting me.

Mary's problem was just the opposite:

"I blurted out almost everything that came into my mind, regardless of how it might have affected Richard. If I was angry about something, I seldom kept it a secret. Richard never had to guess what I was feeling. I told him in no uncertain terms, sometimes in loud, angry, insulting, and belittling tones."

Neither of us was thinking about the other; we were each concerned about ourselves. Mary's attack would send me deeper into my shell for protection. But the more I retreated, the more forceful she became, desperately seeking to have her needs met and to be understood. We knew that if our marriage was ever to improve, we had to work on our communication skills.

For openers, I knew I had to open up, admit what I was thinking, say what I was feeling, and allow her into my world.

Now when I come home in the evening, I try to sit down for 20 minutes and rehash with her some of the events of the day—not only to recount the events themselves, but also to relate my feelings about them. For instance, if I have had the opportunity to introduce someone to Christ, I give the details and describe my joy. If I have done something poorly, I explain it honestly and admit my anguish.

Honest communication does not mean that we must blurt out everything that comes into our minds. Some things are unmistakably hurtful and are better left unsaid. But it *does* mean that we begin to develop a greater transparency about our thoughts and feelings.

How Much Should We Tell?

One good rule is to disclose whatever affects our attitudes or actions toward our mates. If they are feeling the effects of our temper or mood, they have a right to know what is on our minds. If I am irritated with Mary because she has snapped at me, then she has a right to know. And I have an obligation to tell her about it in a kind, calm manner—without laying the blame on her.

Honestly admitting what is on my mind has helped make me more accountable to Mary, and this has helped me grow emotionally and spiritually. As I have grown, the pages of my mind have opened wider, contributing to a greater intimacy between us.

As Mary and I continue to open ourselves more to one another, share our souls, and then eagerly listen to each other, we are drawn closer together in an exciting and mutually satisfying bond of intimacy.

Richard and Mary Strauss are authors and seminar leaders. Excerpted from *When Two Walk Together*, ©1988 by Richard and Mary Strauss. Published by Here's Life Publishers, Inc. Used by permission.

4

Lonely Husbands, Lonely Wives

Dennis Rainey

My daughter, Ashley, slipped into my study and asked me what I was writing about. "Isolation," I replied. "Do you know what that means?"

"Oh," said my blue-eyed, blonde-haired, freckle-faced 10-year-old, "that's when somebody excludes you."

I may be a bit prejudiced, but I like Ashley's answer better than the dictionary's definition, which says isolation is "the condition of being alone, separated, solitary, set apart."

Ashley's answer is a profound observation on human relationships. Husbands excluding wives and wives excluding husbands is exactly what happens when loneliness and isolation infect a marriage.

When you're excluded, you have a feeling of distance. You experience a lack of closeness and little real intimacy. You can share a bed, eat at the same dinner table, watch the same TV, share the same checking account, and parent the same children—but you can still be alone.

You may have sex, but you don't have love; you may talk, but you don't communicate. You may live together, but you don't share life with one another.

Because an alarming number of good marriages are unaware of this problem, I will venture a bold premise: *Your marriage naturally moves toward a state of isolation.* Unless you lovingly and energetically nurture your marriage, you will begin to drift away from your mate.

In 1976, I began the Family Ministry, which is part of Campus Crusade for Christ. We've now held hundreds of Family Life conferences all over the world. From the comments we've received, it's obvious to us that isolation is the number-one problem in marriage relationships today.

Periods of Pruning

One of our foundational Homebuilders Principles is: *If you do not tackle your problems together with God's help, you will fall apart.*

Lloyd Shadrach is a good friend and a leader in our ministry to families. He is sensitive to the lessons God has for him. Recently, Lloyd took a walk after a fierce thunderstorm rumbled through Little Rock, Arkansas. As he walked down a road lined with massive, towering oak trees, he had to step over dead limbs that had been blown down. Decaying branches—once lodged amidst the greenery above—now littered the landscape below.

"It was as though God was giving me a personal object lesson of what 'storms' can do in our lives," said Lloyd. "In the middle of the storm, when the wind is gusting, the lightning is popping, and the storm clouds are getting darker, it's difficult to believe our troubles are purposeful. But God may allow a storm in our lives to clear out the dead wood so new growth can occur. Isn't it interesting how fresh the air feels after a storm is over? Sort of unused."

As Lloyd and I talked, I couldn't help but think about the dead wood—several cords of it—that has been blown out of my life. One of the most important things my wife, Barbara, and I have learned from these storms is that God is interested in our growth. He wants us to trust Him in the midst of the storms. He wants us to grow together as a couple and not fall apart.

However, I've seen marriages die from these periods of pruning:

• A child drowns in a swimming pool. The mother blames herself, then abruptly turns on her husband.

• A husband loses a job. The subsequent financial troubles cause his wife to stop believing in him. Their disappointment in each other causes them to retreat from meeting one another's needs.

• An unplanned pregnancy and increased pressures at work provoke a husband to question his commitment to the marriage.

What most couples don't realize is that trials represent an opportunity for them to sink their roots deeper and to gain stability in their relationship.

Once, scientist Lord Kelvin was lecturing his students on an experiment that failed to come off as planned. "Gentlemen, when you are face to face with a difficulty, you are up against a discovery," he said. As inevitable storms rumble through our lives, it's imperative that we turn to one another and not *against* one another.

How Couples Fail to Handle Trials

Families fail to respond properly to adversity in two major ways. First, and most typically, *they fail to anticipate the trials and problems that will come.* Somehow they think none of that will happen to them, but they are mistaken.

A well-known saying reminds us that nothing is sure in life except death and taxes. To those two old foes, you can add troubles. As I read recently, "The man whose problems are all behind him is probably a school bus driver."

Second, when troubles do hit, *many couples simply don't know how to respond.* The trauma brought by the problem is not the real issue. The real issue is the response the couple makes to that trauma.

According to studies conducted by Dr. Mavis Heatherington, 70 percent of marriages in which a child dies or is born deformed end in divorce within five years.

Why does this happen? Couples simply have no strategy for living that goes beyond romance. They don't know how to hold their relationship together and even make it stronger during that desperate period of suffering and pain.

Part of the strategy for facing troubles is to realize that God allows difficulties in our lives for many reasons. I'm not saying He causes difficulties, but I do believe He allows them. Malcolm Muggeridge of Great Britain once wrote:

> Contrary to what might be expected, I look back on experiences that at the time seemed especially desolating and painful with particular satisfaction. Indeed, I can say with complete truthfulness that everything that I have learned in my 75 years in this world, everything that has truly enhanced and enlightened my experience, has been through affliction and not through happiness.

I was just ending a Family Life Conference in Dallas when a trim, well-muscled man greeted me. He told me he was a Green Beret.

Apparently, the seminar had touched a nerve with him. "Dennis, in the the Green Berets we train over and over and then over and over again," he began. "We repeat some exercises until we are sick of them, but our instructors know what they are doing. They want us so prepared and finely trained that when trials and difficulties come on the battlefield, we will be able to fall back upon that which is second nature to us. We literally learn to do things by reflex action."

I realized I'd just heard a great illustration of how Christians should face marriage together. We should be so well trained in God's plan that our reaction to crises and difficulties will be an automatic reflex, not a panicky fumbling around. If we wait until a crisis hits and then turn to the Scriptures, we won't be prepared—and we'll be more susceptible to the enemy.

The Best Way to Handle Trouble

If there's a simple principle for handling problems, it's contained in these five words: "Give thanks in all circumstances" (1 Thessalonians 5:18).

This isn't a simplistic excuse to put your head in the sand and ignore reality. On the contrary, I believe it's the key to dealing with the storms life can bring your way—and that includes the little things as well as the big upheavals and challenges.

If we want to practice giving thanks in everything, we have to ask ourselves: Is God really involved in the details of my life? Could God possibly want to teach me something through a flat tire, a kid's runny nose, or a toy-strewn floor? Does He really want to be part of every moment of my day, or is He willing to settle for the 9:30 slot on Sunday mornings?

Giving thanks in all things expresses faith. Those five little words express our belief that *God knows what He is doing*. And that He can be trusted. As Martin Lloyd-Jones put it: "Faith is the refusal to panic."

Don't Lose Your Perspective

One summer, we lived out of suitcases for seven weeks on the road. It definitely was not easy to give God thanks in everything. On the way to Colorado for a conference, we lost our billfold and purse and had to spend the night in a leaky tent in the middle of a thunderstorm.

When we finally arrived in Fort Collins for the training conference, we questioned whether the Lord really wanted us to start a ministry to families.

Then, a couple of days later, a flash flood swept through Big Thompson Canyon, just a few miles from our training site. It was the worst flash flood in Colorado's history. More than 100 people lost their lives, including seven fellow Campus Crusade for Christ staff women. Twenty-eight other Campus Crusade women narrowly escaped a 20-foot wall of water by going up the side of a canyon in total darkness.

As news of the disaster sank in, Barbara and I realized we really didn't have any problems at all. We had our lives and the privilege of serving the King of kings and Lord of lords. We understood that God has all kinds of ways of teaching His children valuable lessons. No matter what the circumstances might be, there is always something to be thankful for.

Dennis Rainey lives in Little Rock, Arkansas, with his family. Adapted from *Lonely Husbands, Lonely Wives*, ©1989 by Dennis Rainey. Published by Word, Inc., Dallas, Texas. Used by permission.

5

Becoming One

Dr. James C. Dobson

N ot long ago, I was spinning the channel selector on our television set and paused momentarily to watch the "All New Newlywed Game." It was a bad decision.

Bob Eubanks, the show's host, posed a series of dumb questions to a lineup of flaky brides whose husbands were "sequestered backstage in a soundproof room." He challenged the women to predict their husbands' responses to inquiries that went something like this:

"Where was the exact spot your husband saw you stark naked for the first time?"

"If you and your husband ever separated, which of his friends would be the first to make a pass at you?"

"How would you describe the first time you and your husband made 'whoopee,' using these TV terms: First Run, Rerun, or Canceled?"

"Where is the last place you would have, if you could have, made love?"

Without the least hesitation, the women blurted out frank answers to these and other intimate questions. At times I felt I shouldn't be watching, and indeed, past generations would have blushed and gasped at the candor. But Eubanks was undaunted.

He then asked the women to respond to this question: "What kind of insect does your husband remind you of when he's feeling romantic?" If you think the question was ridiculous, consider the answer given by one female contestant. She replied, "A bear." When her husband realized his wife couldn't tell an insect from a mammal, he pounded her frantically with his answer card. She said, "Wellll . . . I didn't know!"

Ingredients of Instability

It has been said that television programming reflects the values held widely within the society it serves. Heaven help us if that is true in this instance. The impulsive responses of the newlyweds revealed their embarrassing immaturity, selfishness, hostility, vulnerability, and sense of inadequacy.

These are the prime ingredients of marital instability, and too commonly, divorce itself. An army of disillusioned ex-husbands and ex-wives can attest to that fact all too well.

For every 10 marriages occurring in America today, five will end in bitter conflict and divorce. That is tragic . . . but have you ever wondered what happens to the other five? Do they sail blissfully into the sunset? Hardly! According to clinical psychologist Neil Warren, who has appeared on my "Focus on the Family" radio program, all five will stay together a lifetime, but in varying degrees of disharmony.

He quoted the research of Dr. John Cuber, whose findings were published in a book entitled The Significant Americans. Cuber learned that some couples will remain married for the benefit of the children, while others will pass the years in relative apathy. Incredibly, only one or two out of 10 will achieve what might be called "intimacy" in the relationship.

By intimacy, Dr. Warren is referring to the mystical bond of friendship, commitment, and understanding that almost defies explanation. It occurs when a man and woman, being separate and distinct individuals, are fused into a single unit which the Bible calls "one flesh."

I'm convinced the human spirit craves this kind of unconditional love and experiences something akin to "soul hunger" when it cannot be achieved. I'm also certain that most couples expect to find intimacy in marriage, but somehow it usually eludes them.

To those who are anticipating a wedding in the near future, and to couples experiencing their first few years as husbands and wives, let me ask you these tough questions: When the story of your family is finally written, what will the record show? Will you cultivate an intimate marriage, or will you journey relentlessly down the road toward divorce proceedings, with consequent property settlement, custody battles, and broken dreams? How will you beat the odds?

Fortunately, you are not merely passive victims in the unfolding drama of your lives together. You *can* build a stable relationship that will withstand the storms of life.

Collision with Reality

I heard a story about a young man who fell in love with a pretty young lady. He took her home to meet his mother before asking her to marry him. But alas, his mother disliked the girl intensely and refused to give her blessings. Three times this happened with different candidates for marriage, leaving the young man exasperated.

Finally, in desperation, he found a girl who was amazingly like his mother. They walked, talked, and even looked alike. *Surely my mother will approve of this selection,* he thought. With great anticipation, he took his new friend home to be considered . . . and behold, his father hated her!

This young man had a problem, to be sure, but he is not the only one. Finding the right person to love for a lifetime can be one of the greatest challenges in living. By the time you locate a sane, loyal, mature, disciplined, intelligent, motivated, chaste, kind, unselfish, attractive, and godly partner, you're too worn out to care. Furthermore, merely *locating* Mr. or Miss Marvelous is only half of the assignment; getting that person interested in you is another matter.

The difficulties of identifying and attracting the right partner are graphically illustrated by current statistics on family breakups. In 1986, there were 2.4 million divorces in the United States. What a tragedy! The average duration of those ruined marriages was only seven years—and half of them disintegrated within three years after the wedding. How could this be true?

Not one of those couples anticipated the conflict and pain that quickly settled in. They were shocked . . . surprised . . . dismayed. They stood at the altar and promised to be faithful forever, never dreaming they were making the greatest mistake of their lives. For years I have asked myself why this collision with reality occurs and how it can be avoided.

Part of the problem is that many couples come into marriage having had no healthy role models in their formative years. If 50 percent of the families are splitting up today, that means half of the marriageable young adults have seen only conflict and disillusionment at home. They have felt the apathy and heard the piercing silence between their parents. It's no wonder that today's newlyweds often sputter and fumble their way through early married life.

Among these destructive customs is the tendency for young men and women to marry virtual strangers. Oh, I know a typical couple talks for countless hours during the courtship period, and they believe they know each other. But a dating relationship is designed to *conceal* information, not reveal it. Each partner puts his or her best foot forward, hiding embarrassing facts, habits, flaws, and temperaments.

Consequently, the bride and groom enter into marriage with an array of private assumptions about how life will be lived after the wedding. Major conflict occurs a few weeks later when they discover that they differ radically on what each partner considers to be nonnegotiable issues. The stage is then set for arguments and hurt feelings that never occurred during the courtship experience.

For this reason, I strongly believe in premarital counseling. Each engaged couple, even those who seem perfectly suited for one another, should participate in *at least* six to 10 sessions with someone who is trained to help them prepare for marriage. The primary purpose of these encounters is to identify the assumptions each partner holds and to work through the areas of potential conflict.

Questions to Consider

The following questions are a few of the issues that should be evaluated and discussed in the presence of a supportive counselor or pastor:

Where will you live after getting married?

Will the bride work? For how long?

Are children planned? How many? How soon? How far apart?
Will the wife return to work after babies arrive? How quickly?
How will the kids be disciplined? Fed? Trained?
What church will you attend?
Are there theological differences to be reckoned with?
How will your roles be different?
How will you respond to each set of in-laws?
Where will you spend Thanksgiving and Christmas holidays?
How will financial decisions be made?
Who will write the checks?
How do you feel about credit?
Will a car be bought with borrowed money? How soon? What
    kind?
How far do you expect to go sexually before marriage?
If the bride's friends differ from the groom's buddies, how will you
    relate to them?
What are your greatest apprehensions about your fiancé(e)?
What expectations do you have for him/her?

The list of important questions is almost endless, and many surprises turn up as they are discussed. Some couples suddenly discover major problems that had not surfaced until then . . . and they agree to either postpone or call off the wedding. Others work through their conflicts and proceed toward marriage with increased confidence. All have benefited from the effort.

Someone has said: The key to a healthy marriage is to keep your eyes wide open before you wed and half closed thereafter. I agree.

Noted counselor and author Norman Wright is perhaps the guru of premarital counseling, having written and spoken extensively on this subject. He discussed his views during a recent interview on my radio broadcast and made several additional observations.

• Couples should not announce their engagement or select a wedding date until at least half of the counseling sessions are completed. That way they can gracefully go their separate ways if unresolvable conflicts and problems emerge.

• Couples need to think through the implications of their decisions regarding children. For example, when an engaged man and woman indicate they intend to have three children, each three years apart, they will not be alone at home for 26 more years once the first child is born! Couples often are stunned at hearing this. They then proceed to talk about how they will nurture their relationship and keep it alive throughout the parenting years. It is a healthy interaction.

• Spiritual incompatibility is very common in couples today. The man and woman may share the same belief system, but one partner is often relatively immature and the other is well-seasoned. In those instances, couples should pray together silently for three to four minutes a day, and then share their prayers out loud.

After they are married, Wright recommends they ask one another each morning, "How can I pray for you today?" At the end of the day, they are instructed to ask again about the issues raised in the morning and to pray about them together. That's not a bad way to handle stress in any relationship!

• Another frequent source of conflict is the continuation of parental dependency in one or both partners. This problem is more likely to occur if an individual has never lived away from home. In those cases, additional measures must be taken to lessen the dependency. Living arrangements are changed so that the person cooks his/her own meals, does the laundry, and exercises independence in other ways. Parental overprotection can be a marriage killer if not recognized and handled properly.

• Many loving parents today are paying for premarital counseling as a gift to an engaged son or daughter. I think this is an excellent idea—and may be the greatest contribution mothers and fathers will ever make to long-term marriage in the next generation.

Excerpted from *Love for a Lifetime*, © 1987 by Dr. James C. Dobson. Published by Questar Publishers. Used by permission.

♥6

It's Always
Courting Time

Zig Ziglar

*I*n marriage, little things make big differences. For example, fellows, there's a dramatic difference in referring to your one and only as a "vision" instead of a "sight."

There's also just a day's difference in time, but light years of difference in meaning, between telling your beloved she looks like the first day of spring compared to the last day of a long winter.

On the serious side, 17 years ago I went on a diet and exercise program. I lost 37 pounds in 10 months by losing 1.9 ounces per day. People who are successful at whatever they do reach their objectives by a series of little things they do every day. If you will do the little things I am suggesting (on a daily basis), they will make a big difference in your relationship with your mate.

Some of these "little" things will make a dramatic difference almost immediately, while others will take time. A lot depends on the condition of the marriage at the moment, and whether you take the steps grudgingly because you have "nothing to lose" or you take them with a loving, expectant attitude. But please hear this: Regardless of your attitude when you start the procedures, the process of doing them *will* ultimately produce results.

Start Today

When our son, Tom, was in the fifth grade, he brought home this little formula for a happy marriage:

> Take one cup of love, two cups of loyalty, three cups of forgiveness, four quarts of faith, and one barrel of laughter. Take love and loyalty and mix them thoroughly with faith; blend with tenderness, kindness, and understanding. Add friendship and hope. Sprinkle abundantly with laughter. Bake it with sunshine. Wrap it regularly with lots of hugs. Serve generous helpings daily.

The Golden Rule clearly says you should do unto your mate as you want your mate to do unto you. Please notice the instructions say we are to initiate the action. Here are some of those action steps:

• **Spoil each other.** There really are many instances when husbands and wives need to "spoil" each other. Wives, you can bake him a cake or prepare a special dish you know he enjoys. Whether you and the kids enjoy it isn't important; you prepare that dish just because you love him. If you send him off to work with a cold lunch, be sure to include a warm note in that lunch to warm it up a bit. Just let him know you'll be looking forward to seeing him when he gets home in the evening. Not a big deal, but it can make a great deal of difference.

Fellows, a little thing like calling your mate during a coffee break is no big deal, but over a period of time, little things do make a big difference. A simple little thing, even like regularly opening the car door for your wife, can make a big difference.

In the 43 years we've been married, I honestly don't believe my wife has opened her own car door a dozen times when we've been together. Now, obviously, she's physically capable of opening it, but I personally feel good when I'm privileged to do such a simple little thing like opening that door for her. It serves as a constant reminder to me that she is important, and I want to be constantly aware of taking the action steps that say, "I love you."

Look for those things that can ease your mate's path and make your own life and marriage happier.

If the husband and wife are both working outside the home, then dealing with the children, preparing the evening meal, and doing the laundry do not fit under the category of "woman's work." These tasks are family responsibilities and, I might add, *opportunities*. If the family includes a husband and a wife and a couple of children, that means four people created the work. If four people created disorder in the home, but only one is doing the work, an impossible burden is placed on that one. You function as a team. It's that simple.

• **Express appreciation.** When your mate does *anything* that makes your trip through life a little easier, a sincere "thank you" is important and appreciated. If you expect your mate to do something because it's his or her "job" or responsibility, the odds are long that it will be done reluctantly, poorly, or not at all. If you express appreciation, results are far better.

Those little thank-yous are indications of *class*. My mother told me many times that we might not all be rich and smart, but we can all be kind and courteous.

And for what it's worth, as I've dealt with leaders in business, industry, and government, I've noted, almost without exception, that the higher in the organization, the more courteous and polite these men and women are. The 16th-century French writer De Sales was right: "Nothing is so strong as gentleness; nothing so gentle as real strength."

• **Know when to apologize.** Many times husbands and wives act considerably less than mature (would you believe *childishly* and *selfishly?*) when they hit a snag in their relationship, and stubborn pride (*hardheaded arrogance* might be more accurate) erects a serious roadblock in the marriage.

For example: The husband says, "If she showed more affection, I'd come home earlier."

Meanwhile the wife says, "If he came home earlier, I'd show more affection."

Remember, when disagreements take place, who makes the move

to make up isn't important. The one who *makes* the move demonstrates the greater maturity and love, as well as the greater concern that the marriage not only will survive, but thrive in an atmosphere of love and understanding. And when *you* are wrong, the most important words in your vocabulary are, "I'm sorry, Honey. Will you forgive me?"

• **Take time out.** A friend of mine received an unusual present from his wife for their anniversary. When he arrived home from the office one Friday, very tired from a hard day, she said, "Honey, we need to run one errand before dinner this evening." Giving him directions by a circuitous route, she took him to one of the nicest hotels in Dallas, where she had arranged a special weekend of relaxation together.

Similar options may include fixing your spouse his favorite food or taking her to that incredible restaurant she's always wanted to visit.

None of these approaches fits the budget of all families, but husbands, here's an affordable challenge. On a regular basis, especially if you have small children, give your wife complete freedom for the day. Get up early with the kids, prepare their breakfast, and take care of their *every* need. Your wife could visit friends, shop a little, have lunch out, catch a movie, walk in the park, and "live it up" in general.

In the meantime, Dad is back home looking after the kids and gaining a new appreciation for his wife. This approach helps both husband and wife gain a new respect and admiration for each other. The kids win, too, because they get to know their dad much better when he spends time with them doing the things Mom normally does.

With careful budgeting and planning, most couples can squirrel away money for a heavy date or short weekend trip where you can devote 100 percent of your time and attention to each other.

The time for each other is the important issue, not where you spend the time. You can set aside, on a regular basis, time for a casual walk, just so you can be in a together situation. Even an unhurried stroll will open the door of thoughtful conversation, and you'll be amazed at how much a regular 30-minute walk will do for the marriage. From time to time, you need to turn off the TV and devote your time and attention to each other. This assures your mate that he or she is important to you, especially if you look each other in the eye as you talk.

• **Develop a sense of humor.** In our hurry, hurry, rush, rush, do it now, instant everything world, with all the distractions we face, surely one of the most effective tools at our disposal to keep romance alive and a relationship open, loving, and caring is a sense of humor.

I encourage you, as husbands and wives, to do things together that will help you laugh. Interestingly enough, people tell me they enjoy humor, that they like to laugh, and that truly funny things are enjoyable to see. Yet very few of them spend any time developing and using their own sense of humor.

Combine that sense of humor with some old-fashioned optimism and you have two powerful components that will go a long way in a marriage.

• **Know that gifts matter.** We all like to feel important and be remembered on our birthdays, anniversaries, Valentine's Day, Christmas, and other special holidays. But we should also remember those occasions when there are no occasions. Drop your mate a note in the mail, "just because." Pick up a single flower and take it home, "just because."

Call from time to time during the day and express your love to your mate. When you have occasions to choose gifts, choose them with care, thinking of what your mate would really want.

If you're the recipient of a gift you are less than enthusiastic about, let me remind you that behind the gift is a thought, and the person who had that thought is your mate. Your mate chose the gift to please you. So, husband, if she gave you after-shave for your birthday, use it after you shave. Don't leave it on the shelf 'til next year so you can pitch it out during spring cleaning.

If she gave you a sweater and you don't particularly enjoy wearing sweaters, go ahead and wear it occasionally anyway. That's just a gracious way of saying, "Thank you for loving me and thinking of me when you bought this gift."

Wives, if he chooses the wrong color or fragrance, just remember he was thinking about you when he made the purchase. You can truly love him and thank him for that.

When your mate makes a mistake and buys a gift you don't want, please don't do what I saw one lady do. She publicly berated her husband for buying her a dress that was the wrong size and color. She told him in no uncertain terms he should know she wore a smaller size and that green was not her color. What she effectively did was discourage him from ever again attempting to buy her anything.

Please understand that whether the gift is a 10-carat diamond, a cruise around the world, or a two-dollar item, it isn't the gift itself but the thought behind the gift that really counts. As the medieval character Sir Lancelot said, "The gift without the giver is bare."

In short, husbands and wives, don't get carried away with "things" to give your mate, but do give yourself. From time to time, a simple gift or card or—even better—a handwritten love letter shows marvelous devotion to your mate. Its cost is zero; its value is enormous.

By now, you could be thinking courtship after marriage takes a lot of time. You're right, but the return on this time investment is enormous. Not only are the ongoing rewards exciting, but it takes considerably less time to maintain a loving relationship than it does to repair a broken one.

Zig Ziglar is a nationally recognized speaker who lives in Dallas, Texas. He and his wife, Jean, have four children and three grandchildren. Excerpted from *Courtship After Marriage*, © Zig Ziglar. Published by Thomas Nelson Publishing. Used by permission.

❦7

Date
Your Mate

Doug Fields

I love to watch people. My wife, Cathy, and I were recently at a resort. While lounging beside a huge swimming pool, we watched a hundred-plus people tanning, swimming, playing, reading, and otherwise enjoying themselves. I focused my attention on the various couples around the pool.

As far as I could see, the pairs having the best time weren't the married ones. As a matter of fact, most of the married couples appeared rather bored. If they were having fun with each other, you'd never have known it by looking at them.

We watched one couple in their 70s playing around in the water, giggling, splashing, and enjoying one another immensely. I assumed, because of their age, that they were married. But we soon learned it wasn't so—they, too, were just "dating!"

Men and Women Are Different (In Case You Didn't Know!)

I realize that my poolside observations do not constitute a scientific study of marriage. But my simple conclusion is this: Many couples become bored and disinterested once they are married. And this point of view is reinforced by my daily encounters with married couples for whom dating and romance are all but nonexistent.

For years, I've spoken to groups on the subject of creative dating. And the one response I continually hear is, "Those ideas you presented sound like a lot of fun—but I'm married!" I've heard this so many times I'm beginning to believe there's a clause on the marriage license stating, "Once married, you shall no longer date. Furthermore, if you decide to do anything resembling a date, it shall be called 'going-out' and shall never be too exciting!"

If you can empathize with the plight of a partner in an uneventful marriage, or if you have, at times, found your marriage void of romance, you need to understand three simple truths:

1. You're not alone.
2. You can be more romantic very easily.
3. This article will help.

It's your attitude and your willingness to change yourself and your behavior that can make the difference in your marital circumstances. With the right spirit and motivation, you can help strengthen a good marriage as well as encourage a troubled one. Many of the ideas for dating (see page 52) may appear fun, silly, and even outlandish. A few ideas are designed to bring out your childlike spirit and to encourage playful interaction. Some ideas will inspire you toward greater depth in your relationship, while others may make you shudder. Please realize that these are only suggestions—meant to serve as the icing highlighting a multi-layered cake.

The secret to sharing a good marriage can never be a bunch of clever ideas anyway. If you're counting on my suggestions to solve your troubles, you're going to be disappointed. There isn't a quick fix to any marriage, no matter how creative the remedy might be. You can't skip the main ingredients of a recipe and expect the icing to make up for the bad taste and texture of the cake. Good marriages don't function that way, either. They take time and energy.

Unfortunately, many couples have lost the spark they shared before they married and have replaced it with a humdrum routine. Dating and romancing your spouse can change those patterns and can be a lot of fun, but it will require some hard work. Planning and energy are imperative for making good times happen.

Is it worth the trouble? I'm convinced that the lack of dating and romance in marriage is one of the major causes of a broken relationship. Marriages usually don't collapse overnight. They become bankrupt gradually because they lack daily deposits of love, communication, and affirmation.

I recently heard a local congressman tell a reporter that he is willing to do "anything" to help rebuild Kuwait in the aftermath of its terrible destruction. I thought this was an interesting comment. Not long ago, this same man allowed his marriage to fall apart. The physical devastation of Kuwait will be repaired within a few years. But once a marriage relationship is destroyed, it can rarely be renovated. "Preventive maintenance" takes ongoing work—work that must be done sooner, not later.

Successful Marriages Require Our Best Efforts

I find very few people who have trouble agreeing that a good marriage requires hard work. But most people struggle and get discouraged when they try to explain their own lack of dating and romance. There are countless excuses guaranteed to keep you from taking action when it comes to dating your mate. I know all about them—I've thought of several myself:

- What are we going to do with the children?
- I don't have enough time.
- Dating costs too much money.
- I'm too tired.
- There's nothing to do where we live.
- We can't ever get good baby-sitters.
- It's too cold outside.
- I have too much to do around the house.

It's true. We can always think of excuses to avoid doing certain things. I can think of 10 reasons for not getting out of bed in the morning, and another five for not filling my car with gasoline. I can make all the excuses I want to, but eventually the pressures of reality will force me into action.

The urgency of life tells me I'd better get out of bed and get gas in my car. Otherwise, I'll never make it to work, I'll get myself fired, and I'll end up without enough money for survival! I'm forced to do what I should, regardless of my excuses. That's reality.

But as far as my marriage is concerned, the consequences of my excuses aren't nearly as tangible or immediate. If I don't take Cathy out on Friday night, so what? Life will go on. I'll still be employed. I'll still be able to afford gas. I'm not forced to make any special effort toward our relationship because there appears to be no urgency. I can continue not making deposits for a long time before my marriage account dries up.

You don't need to be a rocket scientist to figure out that this sort of attitude lies behind the rapid deterioration of marriages. Our nation's divorce rate is phenomenal. If it continues at the present rate, we won't have any families left by the year 2008!

If you want to add life to your marriage, perhaps even save its life, you'd better do whatever it takes to bring romance and dating back into the picture. As I said, there's no quick fix. But if you're willing to make the proper investments, you'll find great rewards. So, in the face of all the excuses, let's take a look at five important ways you will benefit from dating your spouse.

Dating Strengthens Your Relationship

Relationships are strengthened through time spent together, honest communication, and positive memories. Dating provides all of these. Dating builds up marriages and helps solidify their foundations. Enduring relationships aren't constructed out of fleeting emotions and occasional passion. They are solidly built on quality time spent together, each partner investing in the other.

Cathy and I have a date night once a week. We don't necessarily make every date a "creative date." But almost without exception, our time of shared experience and intimacy brings us closer together. It's not always easy and inexpensive to find a baby-sitter, but we place high priority on our weekly dates. And the value they add to our marriage can't be measured in financial terms.

Dating Enriches Life

Life was given to us by our Creator to be lived to its fullest. And He gave us a great playground we affectionately call "Earth" to use and enjoy while we have the opportunity. Setting time aside to enjoy one another not only pleases God, but it also enriches the quality of our lives. You are bound to be a much better husband or wife when you invest time in your marriage, giving it higher priority than the television set, the PTA, the office, church activities, or the golf course.

Dating Creates Positive Memories

Quality relationships are rich in positive memories. Since our world does a good job of dispensing negative experiences, it's up to us to do an even better job of providing positive ones.

I love to hear older couples tell stories of their early dating. While such events are fun to hear about, imagine how much more enjoyable they were to experience! My wife and I are sure to have disappointing episodes and some regretful moments. But one of our goals is to make sure that our positive memories outweigh our heartaches.

Dating Gives You Something to Look Forward To

Cathy and I view our date nights as sacred. They give each of us something exciting to anticipate. I never grow weary of dating my wife. Actually, when I get depressed about work or tired of the bills or disgusted with the piles of "things to do" around the house, one of the things that best lifts my spirit is the awareness that I'm soon going to be spending special time with Cathy. I eagerly anticipate getting out of the house and being alone with the one person I love more than anyone else.

We look forward to our dates!

Dating Models Marriage for Your Children

One of the best ways we can demonstrate love to our children is by expressing affection to our mates. When children have observed their parents placing priority on dating and romance, they will carry that expectation into their own significant relationships.

Kids need to see quality, loving relationships in a world where those aren't the norm. It's not uncommon for kids to fear their parents will divorce—half of their friends' parents have—and many think it's only a matter of time before it happens to their family. Your dating can relieve a tremendous amount of pressure for your children and set an example they will never forget.

Seeing the Big Picture

Two construction workers were busy working on a huge brick-laying project. A passerby was curious about the future of the building. She stopped the workers and asked, "Just what is it you're building?"

The first worker told her he was simply laying bricks, trying to finish a construction project. When she asked the second worker the same question, he stood and proudly explained that he was helping build a great cathedral. He was able to see the big picture and was excited about the outcome. He viewed his job as a worthy task.

As you think about your own marriage, you might want to answer that same question, "What are you building?" I hope, as you attempt to apply some of these ideas, you'll be proud to say, "I'm building a great marriage, day by day, year by year, brick by brick!"

50 Creative Dating Ideas

I developed this list with the hope that each couple would add or subtract from it. You may find some of the more outrageous ideas helpful in stretching your imagination.

* 1. Sketch your dream-house floor plan, and talk about the possibilities for each room.
  2. Write the story of how you met. Get it printed and bound.
  3. List your spouse's best qualities in alphabetical order.
  4. Tour a museum or an art gallery.
  5. Notice the little changes your spouse makes in his/her appearance.
  6. Float on a raft together.
  7. Take a stroll around the block—and hold hands as you walk.
  8. Stock the cupboards with food your spouse loves to eat. (But only if he or she isn't on a diet.)
  9. Give your spouse a back rub.
* 10. Rent a classic love-story video, and watch it while cuddling.
  11. Build a fire in the fireplace, turn out the lights, and talk.
  12. Take a horse-drawn carriage ride.

13. Go swimming in the middle of the night.
14. Write a poem for your spouse.
* 15. Remember to look into your spouse's eyes as he/she tells you about the day.
16. Tell your spouse, "I'm glad I married you!"
* 17. Hug your spouse from behind, and give him/her a kiss on the back of the neck.
18. Stop in the middle of your busy day, and talk to your spouse for 15 minutes.
19. Create your own special holiday.
20. Do something your spouse loves to do, even though it doesn't interest you personally.
21. Send your spouse a love letter.
22. Build a snowman together.
23. Watch the sunset together.
24. Sit on the same side of a restaurant booth.
25. Picnic by a pond.
26. Give your mate a foot massage.
27. Put together a puzzle on a rainy evening.
28. Take a moonlight canoe ride.
* 29. Tell your spouse, "I'd rather be here with you right now than any place in the world."
* 30. Whisper something romantic to your spouse in a crowded room.
31. Have a candlelight picnic in the backyard.
32. Perfume the bed sheets.
33. Serve breakfast in bed.
* 34. Reminisce through old photo albums.
* 35. Go away for the weekend.
36. Share a milk shake with two straws.
* 37. Kiss in the rain.
38. Brush his/her hair.
39. Ride the merry-go-round together.
40. Dedicate a song to her/him over the radio.
* 41. Wink and smile at your spouse from across the room.
42. Have a hot bubble bath ready for him/her at the end of a long day.

43. Buy new satin sheets.
44. Tenderly touch your spouse as you pass one another around the house.
45. Reminisce about your first date.
46. Plant a tree together in honor of your marriage.
47. Go kite flying.
48. Attend a sporting event you've never been to together.
49. Take time to think about him/her during the day, then share those thoughts.
50. Drop everything and do something for the one you love—right now!

Doug Fields, a popular national speaker, is the author of nine books. He and his wife, Cathy, are the parents of two children and live in Irvine, California. Excerpted from *Creative Romance*, © 1991 by Doug Fields. Published by Harvest House Publishers, Eugene, Oregon. Used by permission of author.

♥8

Love for a Lifetime

Dr. James C. Dobson

M y wife, Shirley, and I have been blessed with a wonderful
relationship. She is literally my best friend, and I would
rather spend an evening with her than with anyone else
on earth. But we are also unique individuals and have struggled at
times with our differences. Our most serious conflict has raged now for
27 years, with no solution in sight.

The problem is that we operate on entirely different internal heat-
ing mechanisms. I am very hot-blooded and prefer a Siberian climate
if given a choice. Shirley has ice in her veins and even shivers in the
spring sunshine. She has concluded that if we can have only one flesh
between us, she's going to make it sweat! She will slip over to the thermostat at home and spin the dial to at least 85 degrees. All the bacte-
ria in the house jump for joy and begin reproducing like crazy. In a few
minutes, I am starting to glow and begin throwing open doors and
windows to get relief. That ridiculous tug-of-war has been going on

since our honeymoon and will continue till death do us part. In fact, there have been a few times when I thought death would surely part us over this difficulty.

What is interesting to me is how many other husbands and wives struggle with this problem. It also plagues bosses and their secretaries who fight over the office thermostat. Obviously, temperature is a common pressure point between men and women. Why? Because women typically operate at a lower rate of metabolism than men. It is only one of the countless physiological and emotional differences between the sexes. It is important to understand some of the other ways men and women are unique if we hope to live together in harmony. Genesis tells us that the Creator made two sexes, not one, and that He designed each gender for a specific purpose. Take a good look at male and female anatomy and it becomes obvious that we were crafted to "fit" together. This is not only true in a sexual context but psychologically as well. Eve, being suited to his particular needs, was given to Adam as "help-meet." How unfortunate has been the recent effort to deny this uniqueness and homogenate the human family! It simply won't square with the facts.

We're Not Alike

Here is a quick rundown of a few differences between the genders:

1. Men and women differ in every cell of their bodies. This difference in the chromosome combination is the basic cause of development into either maleness or femaleness.
2. Woman has greater constitutional vitality, perhaps because of this chromosome difference. Normally, in the United States, she outlives man by three or four years.
3. The sexes differ in their basal metabolism—that of woman being normally lower than that of man.
4. They differ in skeletal structure, woman having a shorter head, broader face, chin less protruding, shorter legs, and longer trunk. Boys' teeth last longer than do those of girls.
5. Woman has a larger stomach, kidneys, liver, and appendix, and smaller lungs.
6. In functions, woman has several very important ones totally lacking in man—menstruation, pregnancy, lactation. All of

these influence behavior and feelings. The same gland behaves differently in the two sexes—thus woman's thyroid is larger and more active; it enlarges during pregnancy but also during menstruation; it makes her more prone to goiter, provides resistance to cold, and is associated with the smooth skin, relatively hairless body, and thin layer of subcutaneous fat, which are important elements in the concept of personal beauty. It also contributes to emotional instability—she laughs and cries more easily.

7. Woman's blood contains more water and 20 percent fewer red cells. Since these supply oxygen to the body cells, she tires more easily and is more prone to faint. When the working day in British factories, under wartime conditions, was increased from 10 to 12 hours, accidents involving women increased 150 percent; involving men, not at all.

8. In brute strength, men are 50 percent above women.

9. Woman's heart beats more rapidly (80, vs. 72 for men); blood pressure (10 points lower than man) varies from minute to minute; but she has much less tendency to high blood pressure—at least until after the menopause.

10. Her vital capacity or breathing power is lower.

11. She stands high temperature better than does man; metabolism slows down less.

And Even More Differences

In addition to these physiological differences, the sexes are blessed with a vast array of unique emotional characteristics. It is a wise and dedicated husband who desires to understand his wife's psychological needs and then sets out to meet them.

Briefly stated, love is linked to self-esteem in women. For a man, romantic experiences with his wife are warm and enjoyable and memorable—but not necessary. For a woman, they are her lifeblood. Her confidence, her sexual response, and her zest for living are often directly related to those tender moments when she feels deeply loved and appreciated by her man. That is why flowers and candy and cards are more meaningful to her than to him. This is why she is continually trying to pull him out of the television set or the newspaper, and not vice versa. This is why the anniversary is critically important to her and why she *never* forgets it. That is why *he* had better not forget it! This need for romantic love is not some quirk or peculiarity of his wife, as some may think. This is the way women are made. Men also need to understand that women tend to care more than they about the home and everything in it. Whether your wife or fiancée has a nest-building instinct or not, I don't know, but for years I have observed this feminine interest in the details of the family dwelling. Admittedly, not every woman keeps a neat house. I know some messy ladies whose mothers must have been frightened by garbage trucks when they were pregnant. But even in those cases, there is often a female concern for the house and what is in it. Husbands sometimes fail to comprehend the significance of this inclination.

Shirley and I recognized that we had differing perspectives a few years ago when we purchased a gas barbecue unit for use in our backyard. We hired a plumber to install the device and left for the day. When we returned, we both observed that the barbecue was mounted about eight inches too high. Shirley and I stood looking at the appliance, and our reactions were quite different.

I said, "Yes, it's true. The plumber made a mistake. The barbecue unit is a bit too high. By the way, what's for dinner tonight?"

Shirley reacted more emphatically. She said, "I don't think I can *stand* that thing sticking up in the air like that!"

I could have lived the rest of my life without ever thinking of the barbecue mounting again, but to Shirley it was a big deal. Why? Because we see the home differently. So we called the plumber and had him lower the unit about eight inches. I recommend not only that husbands try to accommodate their wives on matters like this that concern them, but that wives tune in to their husband's quirks and interests, too.

One masculine need comes to mind that wives should not fail to heed. It reflects what men want most in their homes. A survey was taken a few years ago to determine what men care about most and what they hope their wives will understand. The results were surprising. Men did not long for expensive furniture, well-equipped garages, or a private study in which to work. What they wanted most was *tranquility* at home. Competition is so fierce in the workplace today and the stresses of pleasing a boss and surviving professionally are so severe, that the home needs to be a haven to which a man can return. It is a smart woman who tries to make her home what her husband needs it to be.

Of course, many women are also working today, and their husbands are not the only ones in need of tranquility. This is a major problem in two-career families. It is even more difficult in the single-parent situation. I know no simple solution to those stress points, although I'm convinced that emotional instability and even physical illness can occur in the absence of a "safe place." Creating an environment at home to meet that need should be given priority, regardless of the family structure.

Well, so much for this short discourse on sexual distinctiveness. Not only have I attempted to say that males and females are different, which any bloke can see, but also that God authored those differences, and we should appreciate them. It is our uniqueness that gives freshness and vitality to a relationship. How boring it would be if the sexes were identical. How redundant it would have been for the Creator to put Adam to sleep and then fashion yet another man from his rib! No, He brought forth a *woman* and gave her to Adam. He put greater toughness and aggressiveness in the man and more softness and nurturance in the woman—and suited them to one another's needs. And in their relationship, He symbolized the mystical bond between the believer and Christ, Himself. What an incredible concept!

I say to you as husbands and wives, celebrate your uniqueness and learn to compromise when male and female individuality collides. Or as an unnamed Frenchman once said, *"Vive la difference!"* He must have been a happily married man.

12 Marriage Killers

My advice to young couples stands unchallenged: Don't permit the *possibility* of divorce to enter your thinking. Even in moments of great conflict and discouragement, divorce is no solution. It merely substitutes a new set of miseries for the ones left behind. Guard your relationship against erosion as though you were defending your very lives. Yes, you *can* make it together. Not only can you survive, but you can keep your love alive if you give it priority in your system of values.

Any one of the following evils can rip your relationship to shreds if given a place in your lives:

Overcommitment and physical exhaustion. Beware of this danger.

It is especially insidious for young couples who are trying to get started in a profession or in school. Do not try to go to college, work full-time, have a baby, manage a toddler, fix up a house, and start a business at the same time. It sounds ridiculous, but many young couples do just that and are then surprised when their marriage falls apart. Why wouldn't it? The only time they see each other is when they are worn out! It is especially dangerous to have the husband vastly overcommitted and the wife staying home with a preschooler. Her profound loneliness builds discontent and depression, and we all know where that leads. You *must* reserve time for one another if you want to keep your love alive.

Excessive credit and conflict over how money will be spent. We've said it before: Pay *cash* for consumable items, or don't buy. Don't spend more for a house or car than you can afford, leaving too few resources for dating, short trips, baby-sitters, etc. Allocate your funds with the wisdom of Solomon.

Selfishness. There are two kinds of people in the world, the givers and the takers. A marriage between two givers can be a beautiful thing. Friction is the order of the day, however, for a giver and a taker. But two takers can claw each other to pieces within a period of six weeks. In short, selfishness will devastate a marriage every time.

Interference from in-laws. If either the husband or wife have not been fully emancipated from the parents, it is best not to live near them. Autonomy is difficult for some mothers (and fathers) to grant, and close proximity is built for trouble.

Unrealistic expectations. Some couples come into marriage anticipating rose-covered cottages, walks down primrose lanes, and uninterrupted joy. Counselor Jean Lush believes, and I agree, that this romantic illusion is particularly characteristic of American women who expect more from their husbands than they are capable of delivering. The consequent disappointment is an emotional trap. Bring your expectations in line with reality.

Space invaders. Here, I am *not* referring to aliens from Mars. Rather, my concern is for those who violate the breathing room needed by their partners, quickly suffocating them and destroying the attraction between them. Jealousy is one way this phenomenon manifests itself. Another is low self-esteem, which leads the insecure spouse to trample the territory of the other. Love must be free and it must be confident.

Alcohol or substance abuse. These are killers, not only of marriages, but also of people. Avoid them like the plague.

Pornography, gambling, and other addictions. It should be obvious to everyone that the human personality is flawed. It has a tendency to get hooked on destructive behaviors, especially early in life. During an introductory stage, people think they can play with enticements such as pornography or gambling and not get hurt. Indeed, many do walk away unaffected. For some, however, there is a weakness and a vulnerability that is unknown until too late. Then they become addicted to something that tears at the fabric of the family. This warning may seem foolish and even prudish to my readers, but I've made a 25-year study of those who wreck their lives. Their problems often begin in experimentation with a known evil and ultimately end in death . . . or the death of a marriage. The restrictions and commandments of Scriptures were designed to protect us from evil, though it is difficult to believe when we are young, "The wages of sin is death" (Romans 6:23). If we keep our lives clean and do not permit ourselves to toy with evil, the addictions which have ravaged humanity can never touch us.

Sexual frustration, loneliness, low self-esteem, and the greener grass of infidelity. A deadly combination!

Business failure. It does bad things to men, especially. Their agitation over financial reverses sometimes sublimates to anger within the family.

Business success. It is almost as risky to succeed wildly as it is to fail miserably in business. The writer of Proverbs said, "Give me neither poverty nor riches, but give me only my daily bread" (30:8).

Getting married too young. Girls who marry between 14 and 17 years of age are more than twice as likely to divorce as those who marry at 18 or 19 years of age. Those who marry at 18 or 19 are 1.5 times as likely to divorce as those who marry in their 20s. The pressures of adolescence and the stresses of early married life do not mix well. Finish the first before taking on the second.

These are the marriage killers I've seen most often. But in truth, the list is virtually limitless. All that is needed to grow the most vigorous weeds is a small crack in your sidewalk. If you are going to beat the odds and maintain an intimate long-term marriage, you must take the task seriously. The natural order of things will carry you away from one another, not bring you together.

How will you beat the odds? How will you build a solid relationship that will last until death takes you across the great divide? How will you include yourselves among that dwindling number of older couples who have garnered a lifetime of happy memories and experiences? Even after 50 or 60 years, they still look to one another for encouragement and understanding. Their children have grown up in a stable and loving environment and have no ugly scars or bitter memories to erase. Their grandchildren need not be told, delicately, why "Nana and Papa don't live together any more." Only love prevails. That is the way God intended it to be, and it is still possible for you to achieve. But there is no time to lose. Reinforce the river banks. Brace up the bulwarks. Bring in the dredges and deepen the bed. Keep the powerful currents in their proper channels. Only that measure of determination will preserve the love with which you began, and there is very little in life that competes with that priority.

Excerpted from *Love for a Lifetime*, © 1987 by Dr. James C. Dobson. Published by Questar Publishers. Used by permission.

❦9

"Traditional" Families: Fading or Flourishing?

Gary Bauer

I n the 1950s, millions of American families gathered around
their television sets to watch the Nelson family do their funny
thing. Ozzie and Harriet and their two boys, David and Rickie,
presented wholesome family entertainment for many years. They were
part of the genre of TV shows featuring intact families, including programs such as "Father Knows Best," "Leave It to Beaver," "I Love
Lucy," and other situation comedies.

I doubt if the Nelsons ever thought they would someday become a
symbol for traditional values and lifestyles in the '80s and '90s, but that
is exactly what has happened. Curiously, however, it is not the tradi-

63

tionalists who raise the Ozzie and Harriet banner. It is the other side of the cultural divide that uses them—as an object of ridicule and as a symbol of an archaic way of life.

Along with sneering references to "Norman Rockwell's America," the cultural elite frequently remind us that the model of the traditional family—homemaker mother and breadwinner father—is virtually extinct, and they're obviously glad it's gone.

Daniel Seligman, in *Fortune* magazine, did an analysis of news stories in major papers in 1989. Incredibly, he found 88 instances where Ozzie and Harriet of the '50s were mentioned, and the context was similar in each. As Seligman put it, the usual setting featured a politician "on stage reciting the news that the traditional nuclear family—the kind symbolized by the Nelsons during their marathon stint on black-and-white TV—was dead or dying."

To add credibility to the claims that the family is dying, a manufactured bit of statistical "evidence" began to appear in liberal jargon. One reporter put it this way:

> It used to be so simple, it seems in retrospect. Dad at the office or factory and Mom at home nurturing the next generation. No nightmares that one's child would be abused by someone paid to care. No early morning panic when the sitter doesn't show or baby has a fever. No time-consuming search for a center where the prices aren't pegged to the parent's degree of desperation. And no guilt at missing first steps and first words. But the return of those days is about as likely as a prime-time comeback of Ozzie and Harriet. Less than 10 percent of U.S. families are "traditional"—father at work and mother at home.

The reporter didn't explain her source for the "less than 10 percent" figure, but that number has now become widely accepted as fact. Some writers use an even lower number. John Naisbitt, in the bestselling book *Megatrends: Ten New Directions Transforming Our Lives*, puts it this way: "Today, there is no such thing as a typical family. And only a distinct minority (7 percent) of America's population fits the traditional family profile."

Liberal politicians have made good use of this statistical misinformation in recent congressional debates. Senator Christopher Dodd of

Connecticut, one of the leading proponents of federally supported child care, said, "There are [sic] only one in 10 American families today where you have a mom at home and a dad at work—only one in 10. Ozzie and Harriet are gone."

Even conservatives who ran on a pro-family platform got into the act. Senator Orrin Hatch cited the 10 percent figure as his reason for supporting child-care legislation. It was a very effective argument . . . but a phony one.

It is frustrating to see elected officials, the media, and cultural elites use a deliberate distortion to prove that the traditional family is dead and gone. There is no remorse being expressed in their pronouncements. In fact, their reaction borders on outright glee. But like the rumors of Mark Twain's passing, reports of the demise of the family are greatly exaggerated—often by public officials who should (and do) know better.

Setting the Record Straight

What are the real facts? The Family Research Council, based in Washington, D.C., went to some lengths to determine the origin of this 10 percent figure. We found it refers to the families that have an employed father, a stay-at-home mother, and two—count 'em—two children still at home.

What about the family with a go-to-work father, a stay-at-home mother, and one child? Sorry, they're not "traditional," according to this contrived definition. What if that mother is a full-time homemaker who is pregnant with her first child? Nope. She and her husband don't qualify.

What about the childless couple who plans for the wife to work for two years so they can buy a home and then raise a family? You guessed it. They're nontraditional.

Indeed, Jim and Shirley Dobson would be judged "nontraditional" by this definition. Shirley, a former school teacher, stayed at home and raised their two children for 23 years. She's still there today, but her kids are grown and gone. Sad to say, they're considered nontraditional. Nor do the Bauers make the cut. We have *three* kids being mothered by Carol, a full-time homemaker. We have too many kids! Alas, Ozzie and Harriet couldn't even qualify, now that David is married and Rickie is deceased.

Now let me make clear just how abominable this distortion of truth really is. According to the U.S. Department of Labor, 41.3 percent of all married mothers with preschool children are full-time homemakers. Another 20 percent work only part-time, some as few as 10 hours per week in their own homes. That means 61 percent of all mothers who are married with preschool children are occupied *primarily* in the raising of children.

Furthermore, what does outside employment for the wife have to do with whether or not a family is "traditional," anyway?

Employment is not the key factor. I would define a traditional family as one where husband and wife are lawfully married, are committed to each other for life, and adhere to the traditional values on which the family is based. I can assure you that this model for families is not about to pass from the scene!

Why is this particular statistical distortion so pervasive in public rhetoric today? Because the impact of "cooked statistics" on public policy is significant. As Spencer Rich of the *Washington Post* observed:

> *Once in currency, faulty statistics seem to take on a life of their own, gaining momentum from the tendency of the public, once it becomes aware of a trend, to imagine the trend is moving much faster than it really is. For example, a movement away from the traditional family structure is soon interpreted to mean that the traditional family has almost ceased to exist.*

Even more dangerous is the risk that loving husbands and wives who read and hear that they represent an insignificant minority will begin to question their decisions to forgo extra income and material possessions in order to dedicate themselves to the raising of children. These are the very people we should be affirming for their sacrificial contributions to the future of our nation. That fact was widely understood until recent years.

To summarize, the game being played is to issue spurious statistics to convince the public that the family has disintegrated, that homemaking is a thing of the past, and that committed husbands and wives have given way to a nation of single parents, unmarried couples, and gay partners. That will permit federal money and the other advantages of a national policy to be redirected away from mothers at home.

Now certainly, there are more employed women today than a decade ago, and we're seeing an increasing number of single-parent households. Nevertheless, the traditional family has not passed from the scene—nor is it on its deathbed.

A Final Thought

Let me add a personal comment. In the last decade, I have been able to experience things in the corridors of power in Washington, D.C., that few individuals will ever have an opportunity to do. I have walked the historic halls of the White House, where portraits of our great presidents hang in a gallery of honor.

I have sat at the Cabinet Table and shared with top government leaders my best advice on the great issues facing our country. I have stood in the Oval Office with the most powerful men in the world, and I have flown on Air Force One.

I cherish these memories. But in the quiet moments in my own home, sitting by a fire in my den on a cold, wintry day, or lying awake in the early hours of the morning with my wife next to me, it is not these recollections that flood my mind. Rather, it is the special family moments that fill my memory.

I remember the incredible awe I felt in the delivery room when each of our three children was born, the quiet times with my wife when words were not needed, the pride of attending my daughter's honor-roll breakfast, and the moment when my children chose to accept the Lord as their Savior and walk through life with Him.

In these moments, I am reminded that in a world of siren songs beckoning us to the rocks of destruction—power, lust, money—it is the safe harbors of faith and family to which we must anchor our lives.

Gary Bauer is president of the Family Research Council in Washington, D.C. Excerpted from *Children at Risk,* © 1990 by Dr. James C. Dobson and Gary Bauer. Published by Word, Inc., Dallas, Texas. Used by permission.

♥10

Keeping the Memories Alive

Dorothy Burshek

S hortly before his death, my 67-year-old father said, "Life's over so fast." I wondered about his early experiences that had shaped him into who he was. But it was too late to ask.

As I continued to think about my father, I realized that my adult children would undoubtedly have the same questions about my life someday. I thought of the fill-in-the-blank notebooks entitled "My Life Story" and "Grandmother's Memories" they'd already given me. The books were still in my drawer, unused.

But wouldn't it be presumptuous to write my autobiography? After all, only famous people do that. My life has been an ordinary, run-of-the-mill type without great honors. What could *I* possibly write about?

Still, the thought persisted. Soon I was thinking of reasons why I *should* write. Here are some of the reasons I discovered:

- **Faith-building.** The psalmist said: "I will utter things hidden from of old—things we have heard and known, things our fathers have told us. We will not hide them from their children; we will tell the next generation the praiseworthy deeds of the Lord, his power, and the wonders he has done" (Psalm 78: 2-4).

Our children need to hear that God has always been faithful to us, and that we cannot extinguish His love. Even *thinking* about the times I felt His presence in my valleys strengthened my faith. Reading those accounts could do the same for my children.

• **Significance.** Newscasters often show a series of "little pictures" because they know that will better define the "big picture." Our roles as child, student, teen, professional, friend, spouse, parent, retiree, and grandparent may look like small roles, but they're part of the whole person we've become.

• **Healing.** In the process of recording my life, I learned that much of the pain of my past hurts faded. Writing about my relationship with my father was especially helpful. He and his sister had lived in an orphanage outside Chicago before an Iowa farm couple took him in, solely for his value as a worker. They didn't adopt him or love him. He was merely cheaper than hiring another hand for the farm.

In my childhood, my father's terrible temper so frightened and angered me that, at times, I thought I hated him. In the winter, I usually was awakened each morning by curse words blasting into my room from the basement. I knew that the furnace grate had once again fallen into the flames.

As I thought about that scene, my anger toward my father dissolved when I realized he had built a fire each morning so the house would be warm for the rest of us. I also understood how his feelings of rejection had resulted in his anger.

Getting Started

I took a sheet of paper and headed it with "This Is My Story." Then, as quickly as possible, I randomly listed time chunks of my life. At first, I chose a simple chronological listing: Earliest Memories; Preschool; Elementary School; Junior High School; and High School. But the memories, which only trickled at first, rapidly became a flowing stream. Soon I expanded my list with these divisions:

• **A World That's Gone Forever.** I jotted down images of hollyhock dolls, lightning bugs collected in jars, horse-drawn ice wagons, and piles of autumn leaves burning in the driveway. I listed neighbors who dropped by in the evenings to tell stories and sing "Pennies from Heaven" and "Deep Purple." The visits ended with homemade fudge or popcorn.

• **A Child of the Depression.** Food was scarce at times, and early spring days were fine for digging up dandelion greens (before the yellow flowers appeared). Mother cooked the dandelion with a bit of bacon, and because of her cheerfulness, I thought we ate this dish for nutritional reasons. Stored in these years were memories of food baskets arriving from the church and a glorious Christmas provided by friends who knew we wouldn't have any gifts under the tree.

• **Special Occasions.** The disappointment of my ninth birthday party, which nobody attended, is in this section. All the decorations and food were in place when a summer storm brought torrents of rain that must have been familiar to Noah. Most people didn't have cars and couldn't be out in that drenching storm, but my childish heart was inconsolable. I also listed "Fair Day" in this category. Growing up in Des Moines, I thought the Iowa State Fair ranked just slightly below the Second Coming.

• **Gleaned Messages.** Children learn about life from the adults in their lives, so in this section I listed several messages distilled from attitudes found in my home: "You are free to choose, but check out the consequences"; "Pain is inevitable; misery is optional"; "Be generous with God; He's been generous with us"; and "Enjoy life's humor."

• **Molders and Shapers.** People who strongly influenced my life were listed here. The Sunday school teacher I thought most beautiful reappeared in my memory with buck teeth, a feature that had escaped me in my youth. I also recalled my high school journalism teacher, who helped me develop a talent I didn't know I had. My Girl Scout leader was a great encourager, teaching more than knot tying and tree identification.

• **My Family.** For this section, I recalled stories, scoldings, and conversations. I remembered laughter that revealed Mother's beautiful teeth, and images of Dad sitting on the front porch after a rain, inhaling the ambrosia of wet earth. I remembered Mother singing hymns as she worked around the house. She took me to church regularly and to the adult Bible studies she attended. I took my turn with the adults reading the passages, even though I stumbled over the Old Testament names. When we rode the streetcar home after church at night and walked the two long, dark blocks to our house, we kept to the middle of the street. Meanwhile, she sang hymns and told me we were as safe as the missionaries in Africa.

When I had finished listing memories, I transferred the list to a manila folder, one for each section. These segments of my life became the chapter titles of the written story.

Next, I started writing the stories as I recalled them, without worrying about spelling, grammar, or punctuation. I wrote until the memory was exhausted, knowing I could correct later. To help me choose which events to write about, I imagined a good friend sitting across the table from me, listening as she sipped a cup of coffee.

Jogging a Sluggish Memory

At those times when I needed help in retrieving the past, I turned to old photo albums or called family members. Sometimes I browsed through bookstores and libraries for how-to books on recording family history. Old letters from parents and friends opened up forgotten times, as well as school yearbooks and report cards, especially with teacher comments.

The most helpful library resource I found was the Time-Life Books series entitled *This Fabulous Century*. Beginning with 1900, each volume spans a decade—the music, fads, religious life, political events, and radio programs. Scanning a volume winged me home to the console shortwave radio next to my father's recliner, where we gathered to listen to Jack Benny, "The Major Bowes Amateur Hour," and "Fibber McGee and Molly."

Writing my story resulted in a one-of-a-kind gift that only I could give to my family. As I opened the doors of the past and asked God to help me recall important events, I laughed and cried when I saw the humor and drama in my earthly journey. Indeed, I am a creation from the hand of God, an ambassador for Christ. Together, He and I lived the stories—funny, sad, embarrassing, delightful, painful, and whimsical—that are now a record of His hand upon my life.

Dorothy Burshek gave her three children the volume of her life. She and her husband, Cliff, live in Oklahoma City.

🌱🌱🌱
Memories to Keep

As I've thought of the memories I want to pass along to my children, I created a game to encourage the celebration of specific family events.

Follow these steps to keep those stories alive:

Step One. Decide the special event where you'll introduce the game. It could be a birthday, Mother's Day, or an anniversary, but set a definite goal as the deadline. In my case, it was my folks' 50th wedding anniversary reception in Montana two summers ago.

Step Two. At least two months prior to the event, ask family members to contribute 20 questions and answers about their own childhood. Offer sample questions of what you're looking for.

Step Three. Reword the memories into questions, using creativity and humor. For example, "When we walked to Gossett School, how many miles did we trudge through snow, sludge, sleet, and blinding darkness?"

- Use dates. "What are Mom and Dad's birth years—in two seconds or less?"
- Include little-known facts. "Which grandchild did Uncle Fred teach to drive a clutch pickup?"
- Search school routines. "What two places were favorite winter recess play areas?"
- Recall family meal traditions. "What sandwiches did Margaret serve every Sunday evening in the winter?"
- Think of numerical peculiarities. "On whose 66th birthday did the twins turn 33?"
- List friends and neighbors. "Which neighbor made his own root beer?"
- Remember pets. "What was the name of our dog that had 14 puppies on the guest bed?"

Step Four. Print each question neatly on a three-by-five card, with the answer on the back side. Use the cards as a team game at the next reunion, or read the questions and have the group guess which relatives they pertain to. For a matching game, list the questions on one side of the paper, with the mixed-up answers on the opposite side.

At the end of the party, tie the cards with bright ribbon and present them to the guest of honor. Or you can save them for the next family reunion. The important thing is to have fun talking with your relatives and passing along the stories to the next generation.

—Dorothy Burshek

Days to Remember

If your children were asked to name two times when God did something remarkable for *your* family, could they do it? Or, for that matter, could you?

Through Scripture, there runs an underlying concern that the younger generation will forget—or never hear in the first place—about "the mighty works of God." The most striking example occurred when Israel crossed the Jordan River to begin the invasion of Canaan.

The Lord had Joshua stop everything and appoint 12 men to pile up a monument of stones on the bank. Why? "To serve as a sign among you. In the future, when your children ask you, 'What do these stones mean?' tell them that the flow of the Jordan was cut off before the ark of the covenant of the Lord" (Joshua 4:6-7).

God ordered them to create something visual for the sole purpose of triggering questions from the kids.

Hey, Dad—what's that?

Those rocks? Ah, let me tell you about the day God did something incredible for us . . .

Every Christian family can start a notebook of "memorial stones"—occasions when God showed His love and care and power in a specific way. The longer you reminisce, the more things you'll recall that you *really don't* want to forget—things you want your children to know about and cherish along with you, such as:

- The time you got that job you desperately needed and had prayed for.

- The time a long-resistant relative finally yielded to Christ.
- The time God healed someone in your family.
- The time God supplied a financial need in an unusual way.
- The time an unexpected award or honor came along.
- The time that God spared a family member's life.

This may take more than one sitting as strategic pieces of your family's walk with God are captured on paper. Once the list is created, don't bury it. Bring it out a couple of times each year and add new entries. Every time you do, of course, you can also tell your children a story or two from the past, just as Israelite parents did . . . stories that will delight them and impress upon them that they belong to an *active* God.

—*Dean and Grace Merrill*

Granddaddy Tapes

Thirteen years ago, when our oldest daughter, Joy, was 18 months old, my parents and I began trading cassette tapes of our day-to-day activities to save money on lengthy phone calls. One night, as I put Joy to bed, she insisted on hearing her grandfather again. She fell asleep listening to the most recent tape.

The next night, the same thing happened. When I told my dad about Joy's new activity, he saw an opportunity to have a significant part in the lives of his out-of-town grandchildren.

Soon, he was sending tapes to each child, complete with accounts of what he had done that day and stories from children's library books. When one of my daughters was in the *Miss Piggle Wiggle* stage, he recorded an entire tape of those stories for her.

When one of my sons was having difficulties going to bed each evening, Dad made a tape specifically for that problem. He started the tape by telling my son to "lie down and don't fuss. Just listen to Granddad." Then, between stories, he'd say soothing things. After a few nights of this tape, our son went to bed peacefully.

When our second son was born, Dad sent him a tape of family stories and songs recorded just for him.

When we welcomed a four-year-old foster daughter into our home, Dad sent her a tape, too. Several months later, I took her to meet my parents. As soon as she heard my father speak, our new daughter said, "It's Granddad!"

Today, we have a library of several dozen tapes—ranging from Bible stories to Dr. Seuss to Brer Rabbit—that Dad has sent over the years. I have two teenagers, in addition to the four- and five-year-olds, but they still listen to their old favorites when they're home sick. Granddad's rendition of the Tar Baby story still makes us laugh. And to think that someday my grandchildren will laugh at the same story when they listen to their great-grandfather's voice!

—Diane Rawlings

Need Help with Your Story?

Still not sure how to capture your memories? Marcia Moellenberg of Loveland, Colorado, can help. Her business, Legacy Publications, will turn family stories into a printed book.

"My parents are retired missionaries living in California," Marcia says. "I wanted my children to know them as *real* people. So I gathered family stories, asked my parents questions to fill in the missing parts, and then printed a 20-page book about them—from youth to honeymoon."

Soon, as others heard about Marcia's work, she was asked to pen their stories, too. Thus, Legacy Publications was born.

When people contact Marcia for help, she has them complete a 20-page questionnaire asking about their family, siblings, early childhood memories, fears, and dreams. The answers to such questions as "Who was your favorite relative" and "Describe your favorite room in your childhood home" are woven into a narrative illustrated with photos and art. For many, the questions offer more than just a stroll down memory lane.

"Often their answers come from memories that even the spouse didn't know about. Also, the questions will give the person an opportunity to express thoughts on paper—even painful memories—that he hadn't been able to tell anyone else face to face."

For more information, contact Marcia Moellenberg at Legacy Publications, 1414 Allison Drive, Loveland, CO 80538.

PART TWO

FOCUS ON HUSBANDS AND FATHERS

❦11

Men and Women: More Confused Than Ever

Dr. James C.Dobson

*T*raditional concepts of masculinity and femininity have been battered and ridiculed for more than 20 years, creating confusion for both men and women. These revisions of age-old behavior patterns have produced awkwardness in the relationships between the sexes. Should a man stand when a woman enters the room? Will he please her by opening the door for her? Should he give her his seat on a crowded bus or subway? Have all the rules changed? Is there anything predictable and certain in the new order?

While these questions of social etiquette may seem superficial at first, they are hardly trivial. They reflect much deeper attitudes that have far-reaching implications. We are, after all, sexual beings. Everything we do is influenced by our gender assignment. The first element of self-identity as toddlers comes from our identification as boys and girls. Any confusion at that point ... or in the relationship between the sexes ... must be seen as threatening to the stability of society itself.

Dr. Charles Winick at City University of New York studied more than 2,000 cultures that have existed in world history. He found only 55 where masculinity and femininity blurred. Not one of those unisexual societies survived for more than a few years.

Why not? Because a society can be no stronger than the vitality of its families, and its families are a function of the way the sexes relate to each other. Maleness and femaleness are not merely social niceties that have evolved through time. While customs vary from one culture to another, the linkage between the sexes is a function of powerful forces deep within the human spirit. That attraction must not be tampered with by social engineers with an agenda of their own.

Social engineers love to tamper, however, and they've been tinkering with sex-role definitions since at least 1968. Everything understood to identify womanhood for thousands of years has been held up to ridicule and disdain.

It was remarkable, in fact, how effectively a very small number of radical feminists (remember the early bra burners?) were able to redefine the role of women and reorder the relationship between the sexes. These firebrands have long since been discredited, but never underestimate the changes in social attitude that they inspired. In a single decade, for example, the term *housewife* became a symbol of exploitation, oppression, and ... pardon the insult ... stupidity. How strange!

No Apology Needed

Since the beginning of human existence, women in most cultures have identified themselves with child-rearing responsibilities. It was an honorable occupation that required no apology. How has it happened, then, that homemaking has fallen on such lean times in the Western world? Why do women who remain at home in the company of little children feel such disrespect from the society in which they live?

A partial answer can be found in the incessant bombardment by the media on all traditional Judeo-Christian values. Radio, television, the press, and the entertainment industry have literally (and deliberately) changed the way America thinks.

Many years have passed since Barbara Walters and Tom Snyder hosted a three-hour television special on the subject of women. I refer to it now because the program was so typical of the fare served up to the public in that day. The broadcast was aired on NBC in prime time and captured the attention of the country for one full evening. (What fantastic power for social change has been wrought by the tube!)

I watched Walters and Synder carefully on that occasion, and, in fact, taped the program for future reference. Their stated purpose was to evaluate the world of women at that time, examining the many activities and involvement of the feminine gender. What resulted, however, was a powerful propaganda piece for what was then the new way of thinking.

Women were depicted in numerous work situations, from business ownership to blue-collar jobs. Not once in the three-hour program, however, was the role of the homemaker mentioned, except to refer indirectly to this outmoded responsibility in vaguely derogatory terms. Perhaps 14 million homemakers lived and breathed in this country at that time, yet they were not referenced once in a program dedicated to the world of women. I'm sure the viewers got the message.

The effort to reorder the role of women proceeded on a broad scale, touching every dimension of society. For example, I received a letter about that time from a mother who was curious to learn why her local library had removed hundreds of books from its shelves.

Upon investigation, she was shocked to discover that each volume depicting males and females in a traditional context was eliminated. If a woman was shown cooking dinner and a father was working in a factory, the book had to go. Obviously, no stone was left unturned in the campaign to revolutionize our ideas, though none dare call it censorship.

The courts also played a major role during that era. I remember receiving a call from a physician who was consulting with a major law firm. He asked if I would serve as an expert witness on behalf of Sav-On Drug Company in California. I learned that a suit had been brought against the pharmaceutical chain by a feminist attorney who represented the family of a young girl. The suit charged Sav-On with inflicting great psychological damage on the child because . . . are you ready for this? . . . toys in their stores were separated by probable gender interest. Ten feet above the floor were signs identifying "Toys for

Girls," and in another place, "Toys for Boys."

The attorney claimed, apparently with a straight face, that the girl had been emotionally damaged by being "denied access" to toys designated for males. A psychiatrist actually submitted a statement to the court, indicating the great degree to which the child had been wounded by Sav-On Drug Company. *That's* how far the nonsense went.

This campaign to revolutionize our thinking has lost most of its fire today, and the world has moved on. But make no mistake. The case against traditional womanhood has been heard, and it will never be the same.

The female students at Wellesley College in Massachusetts may not be familiar with the history I have described, since some of them were not yet born when the movement began. Nevertheless, they are recipients of its legacy. When they voted not to invite the First Lady, Barbara Bush, to speak at their commencement in 1990 because she hadn't done anything but raise a family and support her husband, they demonstrated how effectively feminist ideology has been ingrained in the attitudes of the young . . . especially those under the influence of liberal professors on university campuses.

The Role of Men

Not only has there been a revolution in female sex-role identity, but maleness has been turned upside down, too. Apart from the elements of social etiquette mentioned earlier, much deeper questions have been raised. What does it really mean to be a man today? We know it is unacceptable to be "macho," whatever that is, but we're not sure how we're expected to perform. Consider how a young husband might look upon his new role at the beginning of married life. Is he supposed to earn a living for his wife? Well, probably not. She may bring in more money than he. Is he expected to provide benevolent leadership for his family in the major decisions?

Even raising that issue in some circles is a sure way to start an argument. Is he supposed to be stoic and strong or tender, sensitive, and emotional? Alas, is there *anything* that distinguishes his role from that of his wife, and where can he go to find out what is expected of him?

Historically, married men were not so uncertain; they understood intuitively that two family responsibilities exceeded all others in significance. They were expected to *protect* and *provide* for their wives and children. You can be sure they felt strongly about that obligation. If you insulted a woman in the 19th century or before, you would have dealt shortly with her angry husband. He would not have hesitated to lay down his life for her, if necessary. He was the defender of her honor, and she felt secure in his care. He took great satisfaction in what he contributed materially and otherwise to the welfare of his family. It was this masculine identity that linked him to his wife and children and gave him a sense of pride and accomplishment in his manhood.

One of the greatest threats to the institution of the family today is the undermining of this role as protector and provider. This is the contribution for which men were designed, physically and emotionally. If it is taken away, their commitment to their wives and children is jeopardized.

Let me personalize the concept. Within a lifetime of responsibilities and professional assignments, I have drawn the greatest satisfaction from the fact that I have cared for each member of my family for more than 30 years. I have worked hard to provide necessities and a few luxuries for them. I have watched over them in times of danger, and I have dedicated myself to their welfare. My identity is inextricably linked with that family commitment. If my role as protector and provider had been taken from me, much of the joy in family life would have gone with it.

A Conversation

Permit me a contrivance to illustrate how far we have drifted in our understanding of this traditional concept of masculinity. Imagine, by some magic, a delegation of yesterday's husbands and fathers being transported through time to visit our day and witness the conditions that Western men have come to tolerate. The conversation between then (perhaps 1870) and now might go something like this:

Today's representative speaks first. He says:

"Our purpose, gentlemen, will be to show you the features of our culture in the 1990s, which differ most radically from yours. And in some instances, the picture will not be a pretty one. Ours is a very violent society, for example. In the United States alone, more than 90,000 women are brutally raped every year. One in three adult females living in certain cities will be ravaged during her lifetime. One in every five

college women is raped on campus . . . usually by someone
she knows. This is a disgrace in our time."

"What?" they would reply in disbelief. "That is worse than
a wartime experience. What is being done to stop it?"

"Very little, I'm afraid."

"What punishment befalls those who are apprehended?"

"Well, most offenders are never caught. Of those who
are, many are never convicted. Only 16 percent will serve
time in prison."

"What do you do with those who are proved guilty? Do
you shoot or hang them?"

"Oh, no! Some spend less than a year in jail, and then
they are set free. Others may be incarcerated for as long as
15 years before being released."

"Released?!! What's to keep them from harming women
again?"

"Unfortunately, many do just that."

"Why do so many men want to rape and kill women?"

"There are many reasons. Some boys grow up very angry
at women. But also, we live in a provocative society. Are
you familiar with the pornography that is available widely
today?"

"No. Does it show women partially clothed?"

"Far worse, I'm afraid. It depicts nude women being bru-
talized in every imaginable way. They are shown being violated with blunt instruments, hanging from trees, and being
murdered with knives, guns, ropes, etc. Every immodesty is
depicted in color and bloody realism."

"I can't breathe! How could such things be? And you say
this material is legal and widely disseminated?"

"Yes, teenagers are the most frequent buyers of it. And in
some countries . . . Australia, for example . . . the same
type of material focusing on *children* is legal."

"You don't mean the public would tolerate such things?"

"I'm afraid so. Australians don't seem offended by it or
by the knowledge that real children are abused by the
photographers. A brisk child pornography business goes on

in North America, too, although it is technically illegal. It was largely ignored in the United States until 1983, but it still generates millions of dollars in sales under the counter."

"Why? Tell us why."

"Obviously, it's not a high priority matter with our legislatures and court system."

"And most of those people are men?"

"Yes, the overwhelming majority are men. They are determined to protect the civil rights of the pornographers."

"What about the civil rights of your women and children? What kind of men would permit such abuse? What has happened to manhood? We would give our lives to protect our loved ones."

"Yes, we've read about your commitment in our history books. Surprisingly, not everyone admires your approach to family life. Some refer to you as chauvinists. That means you are patronizing to women . . . that you don't really respect them. One advertisement tells women they've come a long way since the oppression of your day."

"Oh, really? But your men do respect women, is that right?"

"Yes, but times have changed. The fierce protective spirit toward family life is less intense today. For example, a female minor who is secretly pregnant out of wedlock can receive a legal abortion without parental knowledge."

"Let me sit down. You're telling me that a mother and father would not even be told when their child was violated in that way?"

"That's right. In fact, abortion is not seen as a violation. Even at 13 or 14 years of age, a girl can be transported legally by her teacher or counselor to an agency that terminates pregnancies. There, the baby is drawn from her uterus by a suction device. Not only is parental permission not needed to perform this procedure; they aren't even informed that evening when the young lady comes home. They will never know unless she chooses to tell them."

"But how can parents in that situation care for the girl's health? She's but a child. What if she develops complications from this procedure?"

"If problems develop, the parents may be the last to be told."

"I can't believe fathers would permit someone to assault their daughters in this way. If that happened in our day, someone would be shot over it. What is wrong with the men who accept such outrage?"

"Well, attitudes have changed. Many people today believe the state is really responsible for its children. Parents have a lesser role than in your day. There is a point of view with international adherents, for example, called the 'Children's Rights Movement.' Our position is that boys and girls are entitled at any age to do anything, see anything, decide anything that adults might choose. And when I say anything, I mean just that."

"Anything? You mean, a child could decide to have sexual relations with an adult, and the parents could not intervene?"

"Yes, in Sweden today, it is illegal for a parent to spank a child for disobedience . . . but it is legal for a father to have intercourse with his daughter or a homosexual experience with his son."

"That is sickening. Who would do such a terrible thing?"

"Not many, perhaps. Yet it illustrates how far the children's rights advocates have gone. According to its philosophy, the child is on equal footing with adults. Those who promote this movement want to see boys and girls given the right to vote, travel, choose their own faith, have a guaranteed income, and generally operate independently of their parents."

"Surely, that notion hasn't caught on."

"Not universally, but Western society moves further in that direction every year."

"We think you modernists are a little crazy."

"Oh, by the way, you'll be interested to know that

women are very active in the military today."

"Yes, that was true in our time, too. They served as nurses in the great Civil War, and they rolled bandages and performed other functions."

"No, that's not what I mean. Women today are full-fledged members of the armed forces. When a general mobilization is called, those who have volunteered are required to participate. They don't yet fight in combat, at least not technically, but they are near the battle zone, and they actually help to prosecute the war. Furthermore, many people feel it's only a matter of time before women will be obligated to serve, just as men do, in times of national crisis. It's all part of the equality thing. If women are truly equal to men in the eyes of the law, then they must be willing to fight and die like their male counterparts."

"What if the women have babies?"

"If they're in the military, they have to go. Babies are left behind. When both husbands and wives serve in the armed forces, their children are farmed out to relatives or to someone who will care for them."

"Do you mean a mother of a tiny baby is expected to fight to defend the country, while many able-bodied men stay at home?"

"Yes, millions of male students and others who have not joined the military are exempt. It was the woman's choice to enlist. She must do her duty."

"It is incomprehensible that a man could let a young mother do his fighting for him. But then, your people make no sense anyway. Who would have thought that little more than one century of 'progress' would produce such foolish ideas? The folks back in our day will never believe what we've heard. We will pray for you."

"Thank you."

Yep. You've come a very long way, baby!

It is probably best that no such direct contact between people then and now is actually possible. Past generations would hold us in utter disdain for our failure to preserve and propagate the wisdom of the ages.

Consider that final issue of women in the military, for example. There is a *reason* why men have fought the wars to this point. It has to do with children and societies' acknowledgment of their dependence on their mothers. The image of babies being handed to stay-at-home fathers so their wives could be deployed overseas should be shocking to all of us.

Specifically, there is no more dramatic evidence of the crisis in masculinity today than the fact that men would tolerate even the *possibility* that their wives, sisters, and daughters would do their fighting for them. Isn't that like a man staying in bed with the covers over his head while his wife goes to confront an intruder? Is there no dignity left in modern manhood?

A Crucial Concept

I wish it were possible for me to emphasize just how critical this masculine understanding is to family stability. Sociologist George Gilder said it best in his excellent book *Sexual Suicide*. He makes it clear that single men (as a class) are often a threat to society. Until they accept the responsibility for families, their sexual aggression is largely unbridled and potentially destructive. He writes:

> Men commit over 90 percent of major crimes of violence, 100 percent of the rapes, 95 percent of the burglaries. They comprise 94 percent of our drunken drivers, 70 percent of suicides, 91 percent of offenders against family and children. Single men comprise between 80 and 90 percent of most of the categories of social pathology, and on the average they make less money than any other group in the society—yes, less than single women or working women. As any insurance actuary will tell you, single men are also less responsible about their bills, their driving and other personal conduct. Together with the disintegration of the family, they constitute our leading social problem.

Gilder goes on to say that women, by contrast, are naturally more motivated to achieve long-term stability. Their maternal inclinations (they do exist and are evident in every culture throughout the world) influence them to desire stable homes and a steady source of income. They want security for themselves and their children.

Suddenly, we see the beauty of the divine plan. When a man falls in love with a woman, dedicating himself to care for her and protect her and support her, he suddenly becomes the mainstay of social order. Instead of using his energies to pursue his own lusts and desires, he sweats to build a home and save for the future and seek the best job available. His selfish impulses are inhibited. His sexual passions are channeled. He discovers a sense of pride—yes, masculine pride—because he is needed by his wife and children. Everyone benefits from the relationship.

When a society is composed of millions of individual families that are established on this plan, then the nation is strong and stable. It is the great contribution marriage makes to a civilization. But in its absence, ruination is inevitable. When men have no reason to harness their energies in support of the home, then drug abuse, alcoholism, sexual intrigue, job instability, and aggressive behavior can be expected to run unchecked throughout the culture.

That is precisely what has happened to many inner-city black families. The government pays the bills. Who needs the man? He procreates and disappears. His masculinity has been assaulted, and he takes out his hostilities on the culture that rejected him. It all begins with an unhealthy relationship between the sexes that undermines families and leaves broken lives in its wake.

We must not abandon the biblical concept of masculinity and femininity at this delicate stage of our national history. Not that every woman must become a mother, mind you, or even a homemaker. But those who do must be honored and respected and supported. There should be clear delineation between maleness and femaleness, exemplified by clothing, customs, and function. Men should be encouraged to provide for and protect their families, even laying down their lives for them, if necessary.

Children must be valued as our most priceless possession. Their relationship with their mothers is the most important association in their lives, and it must be given the highest social priority. Boys and girls should be taught that the sexes are equal in worth, but very different from one another. Girls should know they are girls, and boys should know they are boys.

And for the rest of us, self-awareness begins with an understanding of our sexual identity. It must not be blurred by those who have an avant-garde agenda of their own.

Excerpted from *Straight Talk*, © 1991 by Dr. James C. Dobson. Published by Word, Inc., Dallas, Texas. Used by permission.

How to Keep from Being Robbed of Rest

Tim Kimmel

Keeping the average family unsatisfied is vital to our economic system. In order to lure me to a particular product, an advertiser must create a dissatisfaction for what I have . . . or a nagging desire for things I don't need.

Every time I take a shower, I stare at a good example of the persuasive power of advertising. My home came equipped with the standard fixture for a shower. It always managed to get me completely wet and adequately clean. But I kept seeing an ad on TV showing people standing under a special shower head that spun the water around and sent it pulsating over their backs.

The people on the commercial were always smiling and laughing. I thought about the fixture on my shower. It didn't make me smile or laugh. It didn't make my scalp tingle or relax my neck. I had to have one of those shower heads that made taking a bath a holiday.

The new shower fixture cost me about five times more than the one I took off. But my back is worth it, right? I installed this new necessity for happiness about nine years ago. The last time I turned the dial from "Normal" to "Pulsating" was about eight years, 11 months, and three weeks ago. Mainly it has served me as a humble shower. But it does a great job of getting me completely wet and adequately clean.

Essence of Restlessness

Truthfully, I'm grateful to live in a free-market economy. It's a system that offers the greatest opportunities for developing ideas, accommodating needs, and enjoying prosperity. But every good thing has a potential down side. If the best way to keep me coming back for more is to keep me unsatisfied, I'm going to fight a problem with restlessness. And so is my family.

I get a kick out of watching parents take their kids through the checkout lines at grocery stores. If it isn't bad enough that they bought more items than they intended to, they are forced to push their children through a narrow stall that has a million things they could live without within the arm's length of a two-year-old. I couldn't figure out why stores created those checkout nightmares until I began noticing how many people actually succumb to the pressure to add to their 4-foot grocery tab. Those racks filled with hundreds of toys, trinkets, and candy give even the best parent a literal run for his money. ("Yea, though I pass through the valley of the shadow of impulse, I will fear no temper tantrums, because I left my kids at home.")

What I'm addressing is the very essence of restlessness. When we lose control of our expectations, we are guaranteed to be robbed of rest. Yet the culture in which we live makes losing control a foregone conclusion! If I have any hope of enjoying the rest God intends for me, I have to remind myself that I am in a constant struggle with my environment to maintain a sense of satisfaction.

When people fail to discipline their desires, they feel incomplete. A gloomy cloud of inadequacy follows them around. It's difficult to maintain deep relationships with such people—their feelings of inadequacy drain your emotions.

When people fail to discipline their desires, they place unbearable demands on a marriage. Their partner is quick to realize his or her dissatisfaction, and if the partner can't supply all that he or she wants, the partner feels a sense of failure.

When people fail to discipline their desires, they compound stress in their children. An environment where the best is always in the future breeds an attitude that makes the present look cheap.

When people fail to discipline their desires, they accommodate the powers within the world system that desire to control them. A heart that finds it hard to accept its position in life is putty in the hands of the powers of darkness.

When God carved the Ten Commandments in stone, He used the first and last commandments as the supports for the other eight. They were sweeping statements that served as catchalls for the wandering passions of man. If we view these as guidelines for contentment (which they are), we will see why it makes such logical sense to place them in the order in which they appear in the Bible.

The first commandment says: "I am the Lord your God, who brought you out of the land of Egypt, out of the house of slavery. You shall have no other gods before me" (Exodus 20:2-3).

Turning to Him

A focused affection on the God who sets men free is the best way to enjoy a life of balanced love. God is love. He is the essence of its definition. Since love is one of the fundamental needs of man, it stands to reason that we need to begin by loving the Author of love. As we maintain and strengthen our love for Him, we enable our hearts to see the second priority of our existence on earth—people.

The last commandment says: "You shall not covet your neighbor's house; you shall not covet your neighbor's wife or his male servant or his female servant or his ox or his donkey or anything that belongs to your neighbor" (Exodus 20:17).

Coveting has a lot of nasty synonyms: envy, jealousy, lust, greed . . . It starts in our hearts as a seed but gets watered and fertilized by the inevitable pressures on our pride.

Your best friend gets a promotion with a significant pay raise—the seed germinates. The new models for next year roll into the showroom at the car dealerships—the seed sprouts roots. You go shopping with your best friend, and she fits beautifully into dresses that are the same size she wore when she got married 15 years ago. You stare at the size inside the dress you are holding and notice that it's gone up four digits since your wedding day. Ah, the seed of coveting is now starting to show above the surface of your personality.

Coveting is material inebriation. It's an addiction to things that don't last and a craving for things that don't really matter. It forces us to depend on tomorrow to bring us the happiness that today couldn't supply.

The "Greener Grass" Syndrome

I'm amazed how often people end up envying the very people who envy them! A pastor sat back in his chair, listening to the man seated across from him complain about the cross God had given him to bear. This prominent businessman was regretting that he had chosen the line of work he was in. He knew he should be grateful. After all, since he had bought the majority position in the company, its stock had split twice. The P and L statements for the last three years had supplied him with excellent Christmas bonuses. He and his wife had enjoyed visits to Europe, the Orient, Australia, and, most recently, Eastern Europe.

But he fought a lot of guilt.

He had once pursued the pulpit, but, took a side road in seminary that placed him in secular work for good. He went on to outline how much he envied the pastor's knowledge of the Bible and his grasp of theology. He wished that he had the time to sit around and read the Scriptures all day. Furthermore, . . .

The pastor looked past the man's tailored suit to the window through which he could see the two cars parked outside his study. They were the same color, but that was as far as the comparison could go. As soon as this appointment was over, he'd have to take his aging Pontiac home so that his wife could borrow it to do her chores. The odometer broke at 78,000 miles two years ago.

As his counselee rambled on about what a spiritual loser he was, the pastor studied the picture framed on the corner of his desk. His two children smiled so broadly and so proudly. They were too young to be self-conscious. But in a few years, they'd realize what he already knew. Their teeth needed elaborate orthodontic work. But it wasn't going to happen on his paycheck. He kept thinking of all the times that businessmen had said to him, "Pastor, with your skills, you could have knocked 'em dead in the business arena." They never knew that money was one of the biggest temptations of his life.

Changing places wouldn't solve either one of these men's problems. One man was an ungrateful steward of much; the other was an ungrateful steward of many.

The more we measure our significance by other people's accomplishments, the less we'll be able to feel at rest in our daily lives. A rushed lifestyle is only going to bring more successful people to envy, more unaffordable conveniences to covet, and more failures to regret.

Attitudes That Hinder

One way to check your satisfaction quota is to see how you complete a couple of sentences. The second half of these statements can tell all. Let me help by completing them several ways. I may not hit the areas that you struggle in, but the ones I do offer should give you an idea of how to personalize them.

If only I had . . .

> a job
> a better job
> a more understanding boss
> enough money to retire on
> a bigger house
> a thinner waist
> a better education
> a husband
> a different husband
> a child
> a lifestyle like . . .

If only I hadn't . . .

> dropped out of school
> been forced to get married
> had an abortion
> started drinking

            been fired
            run up so many debts
            neglected my wife
            quit that job
            sold that stock
    If only they had . . .
            given me more playing time
            recognized my potential
            offered me the job
            encouraged me to apply myself in school
            supported me in my sports
            been honest with me
            stuck with me
    If only they hadn't . . .
            abandoned me as a baby
            discouraged me
            prejudged me
            pushed me so hard to achieve
            lied to me
            been so interested in making money
            been ashamed of my handicap

If only . . . if only . . . if only. The starting words for unfulfilled expectations or nagging regrets. No one is immune to their destructive impact. Because we are people and not machines, we can't deny the impact of our past mistakes and disappointments. Nor can we turn deaf ears or blind eyes to the many desires of this world that may be out of reach.

A Disappointing Past

Too many people are unsatisfied with where they are because they don't like the path they took to get there. Often the path to the present was not of their personal choosing.

Most people have had to deal with the pain that comes when they don't meet other people's expectations. But all rejection is not equal. The pain of being rejected by a parent or spouse is far more devastating than being rejected for our ideas or unappreciated for our contributions. Some people can't seem to move out of neutral in the present because their primary "reason for living" let them down in the past.

Others put their life in gear but take off in the wrong direction. A disappointing past can throw our expectations out of whack. We suddenly view acquisitions or status as an antidote for the pain of our past. We think that success will prove we can amount to something, that marriage will prove we are worth loving, that wealth will get people's attention.

I remember an enlightening conversation with a plastic surgeon. Much of what he did brought a healthy transformation to his patients. A rebuilt nose could bring an end to years of teasing. A restructured jaw could restore what the disfigurement of an accident had stolen.

"But you know, Tim," he confided, "many people come into my office for a new look, when what they really want is a new *life*."

A key, then, to experiencing lasting rest in our lives is refusing to allow past disappointments to cause us to pursue unhealthy desires. We need to be disciplined at keeping our past hurts in perspective.

I'm so grateful that we don't have to do this alone. The message of the Bible is that God wants to comfort us in our sorrows, fill our voids, and forgive our sins. There is no purchase that will remove the hurt of rejection. There is no activity that will cover the consequences of our negligence. Emptiness and pain need the permanent presence of a God who promised to never leave us or let us down. When our past is handled in a healthy way, we have a better chance of having healthy expectations.

Is It Okay to Dream?

Of course, there is a healthy desire within most of us to improve ourselves and our positions. It is an instinctive quality placed within us by God. To deny it would be foolish, and to ignore it would be sacrilegious.

Certain additions to our lives are capable of giving us a lot of joy. A bigger house could give some badly needed relief from the cramped quarters you presently endure. A graduate degree could offer you a better platform from which to serve people and a better income through which you could accommodate your family needs. An exotic vacation could allow you to make many beautiful memories with people you love. A spouse could give you an opportunity to love and be loved.

There's nothing wrong with these desires.

But if we are going to dream, we need to make sure we are doing two things at the same time.

First, *we need to make sure we are pursuing legitimate goals.* What is a legitimate goal? Anything that improves your ability to love and serve God and people is a legitimate goal.

Is there room, then, for acquiring things that accommodate you? Sure. Beautiful possessions have a legitimate place in a balanced person's life. Possessions can never "complete" you, but they can be rewards that come from hard work and conscientious living. They adorn our lives—but don't make our lives. To pursue possessions in order to fill a void is folly. And if, in the process of pursuing them, we neglect God-given responsibilities, then they are double trouble. Instead of being rewards, they become treacherous obstacles to healthy living.

Therefore, don't be snookered by "The Lifestyles of the Rich and Famous." Material acquisition cannot fill the void within our lives. Status and influence cannot substitute for our need to love and be loved. You want proof? Trace the trail of broken marriages and troubled children that plague many of the people showcased on that television show.

No, there is nothing wrong with living comfortably, dressing well, driving a nice car, or being famous. These are legitimate rewards that always have responsibilities attached to them. But when they become the things that motivate us, complete us, or sustain us, we're sure to wake up one morning and find ourselves empty. Hollow to the core.

Billy Graham put it well when he said that the smallest package he ever saw was a man wrapped up wholly in himself. Undisciplined desires can make small packages out of big people. Jesus said, "Seek first His kingdom and His righteousness; and all these things [the necessities that sustain and satisfy] shall be added to you" (Matthew 6:33).

Bringing Contentment on Board

Remember that I said we need to be doing two things in order to maintain disciplined desires? The first thing is to make sure we are pursuing legitimate goals. The second thing is to *make sure we are making the most of where we are.* You know what I mean. You've seen people who are so busy stretching for the brass ring that they forget to enjoy the merry-go-round.

We need to make contentment a member of our internal board of directors. Give him the freedom to ask the hard questions when you start feeling you need something more to bring you happiness. If you do, be prepared to mumble a lot to yourself. He likes to ask questions like:

- Can you afford this?
- Do you have to give up much of the few spare hours you have left to take advantage of this thing?
- Will this free you up to spend the time necessary to maintain your commitments to family and friends?
- Will this in any way frustrate your relationship with God?

Do you see why people don't want contentment in the boardroom of their hearts? He demands that we place proper value on the things that bring us joy.

An unsatisfied heart in a life with much blessing is sin. As long as we allow this constant craving to dominate our hearts, we will be denied inner rest. As Calvin Miller wrote: "The world is poor because her fortune is buried in the sky and all her treasure maps are of the earth."

The only way we can keep our expectations and desires disciplined is with God's help. A relationship with God that is personal yields a set of desires that are practical. Knowing He loves us and has forgiven us keeps us from wanting the wrong things. By following His example, when He walked the earth, we develop priorities that sustain our hearts, both now and through the future.

Tim Kimmel is a family counselor from Phoenix. Excerpted from *Little House on the Freeway*, ©1987 by Tim Kimmel. Published by Questar Publishers. Used by permission.

❧13

Hedges

Jerry Jenkins

I believe in the power of words, written and spoken. Have you ever noticed that compliments and flattery are always heard? People have reminded me of compliments I have given years ago and almost forgotten. They remember criticism, too, but flattery all the more.

Idle flirting gets people in trouble because the other person needs and wants attention so badly. Not many years ago, I slipped from behind this hedge, not intending to flirt but rather to be funny. It didn't get me in serious trouble, but I was certainly reminded of the reason for my hedge.

Before I get into the story, let me tell you what hedges are. Jesus told parables about landowners who planted vineyards and protected them with hedges. When those hedges were trampled or removed, ruin came to the precious possessions of the landowners. Similarly, we need to plant hedges around our marriages in order to protect them.

Anyway, on a business trip, a woman colleague and I were going out to dinner with a male associate of ours. When she came to pick me up, she was dressed and made up in flashy, coordinated colors that demanded some comment. I should have said something about her clothes, but instead—since she is always a good audience for my humor—I said the first funny thing that popped into my mind: "My, don't you look delicious."

She laughed, and I hoped she knew I meant her color reminded me of fruit, not that I wished to devour her. As soon as our third party arrived, she told him what I had said. He gave me a look that would put a wart on a gravestone, but what could I say? I couldn't deny it, and it was too late to explain.

Men, of course, are just as susceptible to flattery as women. Most people think the man in Proverbs heading down the road of destruction to the harlot's bed had followed his lust for sex. Surely that was part of it, but the text indicates he was also seduced by her words. Proverbs 7:4-5 says, "Say to wisdom, 'You are my sister,' and call understanding your nearest kin, that they may keep you from the immoral woman, from the seductress *who flatters with words*" (emphasis mine).

Everyone knows that funny people speak the truth through humor. They may exaggerate how upset they are that someone is late by looking at their watch and saying, "Oh, glad you could make it!" But beneath the joke is a barb of truth. The jokester has slipped in a little lecture without having had to embarrass anyone by saying, "Hey, pal, we agreed on six o'clock, and now here you come at 6:30. What's the deal? Get your act together!"

But the same thing happens when someone tries to be funny in a flirting manner. A man tells a woman, "Why don't we run off together? Tell that good-for-nothing husband of yours you got a better offer, huh?"

How's a woman supposed to react to that? The first time, she may think it's funny because it's so far out of the realm of possibility. Each succeeding time Mr. Comedian says something like that, it gets a little more irritating. That is, unless the woman has always been attracted to him and has problems at home. Then she might hope there's some truth behind the humor.

Often, there is. The only time a funny flirter is totally putting someone on is when he throws his arm around a particularly old or homely woman and tries to give her a thrill by saying something she's probably never heard before. "Hey, gorgeous! Where have you been all my life?"

Women like that know better than to believe such drivel, but they may long to hear it anyway. A colleague of mine once toyed with just such a woman by caressing her cheek with his hand.

"I'm melting," she said, and I sensed she meant it.

The real danger comes when the man is pretending to be teasing, but he'd really love to flirt in just the way he's exaggerating. A woman may not suspect the truth behind his humor, and if she responds in kind, there is the opportunity for misunderstanding. Or worse, she may indeed suspect that he means it, and then there is the opportunity for real misunderstanding.

Such a tragedy occurred at a church in Michigan where a couple flirted humorously for almost 10 years. They did this in front of everybody, including their spouses, who laughed right along with them. The flirters were never seen alone together, because they never were alone together.

Then came the day when the woman's husband was sick and in the hospital. She needed rides back and forth, and her friend and his wife provided them. No one suspected anything, but on one of those rare occasions when it was just the man doing the driving, the wife of the sick man told him how difficult and cold her husband had been for years.

The flirters began to see each other on the sly until the day came when she told him she had always hoped he'd meant what he said when he teased her about how wonderful she was, how good she looked, and how he wished he'd met her before she was married.

Whether he really meant it was irrelevant now that she had declared herself. The fact was, he admitted later, this was what he had unquestionably wanted all along. He would never have made the first move, however. He had hidden his true desires behind a cloak of humor. A little crisis, a little honesty, and suddenly years of innocent flirting had blossomed into an affair.

I worked at a camp one summer during my high school years. One week, one of the woman counselors, about a year older than me, shared my last name. We were not related and had never seen each other before. When we were introduced, we had not even made much of an issue over the name duplication. While Jenkins is not as common as Smith or Jones, neither is it as unique as Higgenbotham or Szczepanik.

One night, after the campers were in bed, a bunch of us staffers and a few of the counselors, Miss Jenkins included, were watching a baseball game on television. A couple of the guys started kidding Miss Jenkins and me about being married. We were both so young and naive and insecure that we just blushed and hoped the running gag would run out of gas.

For some reason, I had to leave the impromptu party before the game was over, and as I headed for the door, someone said, "Hey, Jenkins, aren't you takin' your wife with ya?"

I got this urge to show the crowd I could be just as funny as them and that I was a good sport, so I turned and pointed at her. "No, but I want you home in bed in 15 minutes."

I was out the door and 10 feet from the TV cabin when I heard the hooting and hollering. I had not intended even to imply anything risqué. I had merely been trying to go along with the joke, and instead of speaking to the girl the way a husband would to a wife, I had spoken to her as a father to a daughter.

Of course, everyone took my wanting her home in bed the wrong way, and with my reputation for enjoying a funny line, I knew I would never live it down. In fact, if I tried to go back and explain, no one would even believe me. They would wonder why I didn't want to take the credit for such a great joke.

The girl was as sweet and chaste as most counselors would be at a camp like that, and the last thing I wanted her to think was that I had been inappropriate and gotten a cheap laugh at her expense. A hundred feet from the cabin, still hearing the laughter, I knew I had to go back.

When I opened the door, no one even noticed me. Something had happened in the game that had everyone's attention. I was glad to see Miss Jenkins wasn't sitting there weeping with her head in her hands. When I called her name and she looked up, so did everyone else, and the snickering began again. I wished they had been laughing at me for saying such a stupid thing, but I knew they were laughing because I had gotten away with such a saucy line.

"Could I see you for a minute?" I asked, and the room fell deathly silent.

I'll never forget her response as long as I live. "I'm not too sure," she said. It was the funniest comeback I could imagine in that situation, and I wish I'd anticipated it. If my original line had been intentional, I would still have always thought hers was better, especially on the spur of the moment.

The place erupted again, and I winced self-consciously, knowing I appeared to deserve that. I was grateful when she bounced to her feet and followed me out into the darkness. I had the impression she knew what I was going to say.

"You need to know I didn't mean that the way it sounded," I said.

"I know," she replied.

"You do?"

"Uh-huh."

"I don't think anyone else understands that."

"Maybe not, but I do. I've seen you around, heard you be funny. That's not your style. At first I was embarrassed and disappointed, but I caught a glimpse of your face as you hurried out, and I knew."

"Your comeback in there was priceless."

"I couldn't pass it up. But I knew you were back to apologize, so I figured I could say something and apologize for it at the same time."

"I'm sorry," I said. "I didn't mean to embarrass you."

"Accepted. I know. And I'm sorry, too, though I admit I did mean to embarrass you."

I laughed and she added, "We Jenkinses have to stick together, you know."

Strangely, we didn't see any more of each other after that than we would have otherwise. She had her crowd, and I had mine. I had learned a lesson, though. I knew to be more careful about teasing in a flirting manner. I also learned how wonderful and forgiving and insightful some women can be. Funny, too.

Along these same lines, I have made it a practice—and can probably list this among my hedges—of *not* making Dianna, my wife, the butt of jokes. There are enough things to make fun of and enough funny topics without going for easy laughs at the expense of your spouse.

One of the reasons for this, besides my memory of how bad I felt about unintentionally ribbing my teenage camp "wife," is that I would never want Dianna to think I was trying to tell her something serious under the guise of humor. We have made it a policy to speak honestly and forthrightly with each other about anything that bothers us.

We give the lie to that pontification that married couples who never fight are probably as miserable and phony as those who fight all the time. We love each other. We don't always agree, and we get on each other's nerves occasionally, but neither of us likes tension in the air. We compete to see who can apologize first and get things talked out. We follow the biblical injunction to never let the sun go down on our wrath (see Ephesians 4:26).

When a group of adult Christians decides it would be healthy to be honest and share some of their most embarrassing or petty fights, we always confess that we'll either have to pass or make one up. Slammed doors, cold shoulder, silent treatments, and walking out just are not part of our routine. I think this comes as a result of being careful with our tongues.

Just as I don't want to make the mistake of flirting in jest or being suggestive in conversation with anyone but my wife, I want to watch what I say to her, too. Scripture has a lot to say about the power of the tongue and the spoken word.

Proverbs 18:21 says that death and life "are in the power of the tongue," and Proverbs 21:23 says, "Whoever guards his mouth and tongue keeps his soul from troubles." In the New Testament, James says that the tongue is a little member, but that it boasts great things. "See how great a forest a little fire kindles!" (James 3:5).

Flattery, flirtation, suggestive jesting, and what we say to our own spouses are all shades of the same color. Beware the power of the tongue.

Jerry Jenkins is a writer-in-residence at Moody Bible Institute. He and his wife, Dianna, are the parents of three children, and they live in the Chicago area.

❧14

Job vs. Family: Striking a Balance

Brian Knowles

George, by his company's definition, is a successful executive with a "Big Eight" accounting firm. Only 32, he's been promoted to partner after 10 years in the trenches.

No one questions his dedication to the job. George leaves the house at 7:00 A.M. sharp for the hour-long commute to work. He often puts in 11-, 12-, even 16-hour days, arriving home well after 9:00 P.M.

When George is not in the office, he's either traveling, entertaining clients at "power lunches," or schmoozing with the senior V.P.s at night baseball games. He often goes to the office at least one day on the weekends, sometimes two. His oft-voiced complaint is that there is too much work to do and too little time to do it.

George's three children are growing up without his notice; they barely know him. His wife fills her days with household chores, errands, and carpools, handling her parental duties like a single parent. Her only diversions are tennis and her late-evening companion—the TV. She and George haven't been to church together in ages.

107

George is not a bad person. He says he loves his wife and children. He is devoted to his parents. But George is married to his job, not his spouse. He's been seduced by a hefty salary, blinded by the power and perks of corporate life. His values are misplaced, and until he gets his priorities in line, he and his family are drifting apart—until they meet again in divorce court.

A New Order

George may be his own worst enemy, but an equally destructive development has risen in recent years: corporate-induced workaholism. As the head of a publications department for a major life insurance company in Los Angeles, I've heard managers say that anyone who puts in only an eight-hour day is "lazy." I've known employees who were *afraid* to leave the office before their boss left, which was never before 8:30 P.M.

I once read a memo spurring employees to shrink the production schedule. "There is no reason why [people] can't turn our work around in one day, not three or four," it began. "Also, I don't want to hear about weekends adding time to the schedule. God made weekends so we could catch up, not so we could fall further behind."

As competition grows more fierce in the workplace, North American companies are being driven to the wall. From New York to Los Angeles, companies are "downsizing" operations—a euphemism for layoffs—and having the remaining employees try to manage the same workload. Because of the erosion of our manufacturing base, firms are forced to offer intangibles—such as service—to compete in a world market. Competition in service means longer hours and greater efforts to meet or exceed the demands of the customer.

Tough-minded young professionals are rising fast because their high energy and aggressive nature are exactly what top management believes will give their firm the competitive edge. Bright, career-minded women are also being promoted as never before. The face of management is changing. It's younger, tougher, leaner, and meaner.

They are also listening to voices who scoff at those who dare work eight hours a day. Some years back, David Ogilvy, in *Confessions of an Advertising Man*, wrote, "If you stay home and tend your gardens and children, I will love you more as a human being, but don't expect to be the first person promoted in your group."

Ogilvy was expressing, in a kinder, more gentle way, what has become the central theme of the modern quest for excellence. Management gurus Tom Peters and Nancy Austin, who travel around the country spreading their gospel of "corporate excellence," explicitly state the price of making it to the top:

> We have found that the majority of passionate activists who hammer away at the old boundaries have given up family vacations, Little League games, birthday dinners, evenings, weekends and lunch hours, gardening, reading, movies, and most other pastimes. We have a number of friends whose marriages or partnerships crumbled under the weight of their devotion to the dream. There are more newly single parents than we expected among our colleagues.

Consider the implications of this incredible statement on the family! These management gurus really believe that those who want to get ahead must sacrifice the family at the altar of work. Company management—and many of their employees—are buying into this mentality.

Last year, *Fortune* magazine published an article, "Is Your Company Asking Too Much?" The author described how a "new corporate style, dubbed the 'high commitment' model, has sprung up, suggesting ominously that your life should revolve around work and not much else." A whole generation of white-collar workers, the article added, are going through life never knowing what a 40-hour work week will be like.

When *Fortune* polled America's top corporate chiefs on the subject, their collective response was: "Stop whining and get back to work. You ain't seen nothing yet!" The CEOs believe American companies will have to push their managers *even harder* to keep up with global competition.

Little wonder that a Lou Harris poll found the work week has increased from 40.6 hours in 1973 to 46.6 hours in 1987. For professional people, the number is even higher: 52 hours a week. Small-business owners and corporate executives put in 57 hours a week.

Jim Gauss, an executive with Witt Associations, a Chicago-based health-care executive search firm, says the work week for managers has increased 10 to 15 hours a week in recent years. "There are a lot of people working 60 to 70 hours a week," he says.

Where are the hours coming from? Time with the family, of course. Parents spend 40 *percent* less time with their children than they did 25 years ago, according to an analysis by the Family Research Council. In the mid-60s, an average parent spent about 30 hours a week with a child. Today, the average parent spends only 17 hours.

This means no time for cheering on a daughter's soccer game, hearing about Junior's fourth-grade teacher over dinner, or strolling through the neighborhood on a twilight walk.

Effects of Overwork

Stress cracks are beginning to show through corporate America. Flesh and blood, after all, have limitations. Workaholism—whether it comes from within or is required—is not only creating havoc with the family, but it's taking its toll on workers' health and mental well-being. I know one manager who's suffered three minor heart attacks, battled a drinking problem, and been through three broken marriages.

Others note that burnout is becoming more and more commonplace in management circles. Companies that practice "survival of the fittest" promotion policies are beginning to alienate—and lose—their best talent. More and more valued managers are bailing out and making mid-life career changes to get out from the relentless pressure to work 12-hour days.

But corporate execs, driven by the demand for short-term performance and the desire to meet a bottom line, are largely insensitive to overworked employees. They simply cast about for "fresh horses." Those who flame out along the way are viewed as weak "non-team" players.

What to Do?

It's time North American companies and workaholics heard a reminder about what our priorities should be. Jesus taught His followers that we ought to "seek first the kingdom of God and His righteousness," and that God would then add the material things.

Should Christian managers and employees abandon the search for excellence? Not at all. It simply means working smarter, doing things right the first time, and above all, getting our priorities in order.

Here are some antidotes for dads and moms who work too much.

• **Pray about it.** Ask God to help you order your life according to His priorities. Examine what's important. If we're not committed to our families, we can't expect them to be committed to us.

• **Think ahead.** Ask yourself how your job will affect your family this year, as well as five years from now. Time does pass more quickly than we think, and we'll soon be facing the consequences of our present work decisions. Occasionally it helps to remind yourself that at the end of life, no one has ever said, "I wish I'd spent more time at my desk."

• **Think through any promotions.** Often promotions come with a corresponding increase in work load and hours. Is it worth it?

• **Have lunch with a family member more often.** If you have to miss family dinner, then invite your mate or a child to lunch. Give that person your undivided attention during that precious hour. This can have a wondrous effect on a family relationship.

• **Block out a few minutes for yourself.** Set the alarm 10 minutes earlier, and aim for a gentler introduction to the day. Taking a short walk or spending extra time in the Word will do wonders for your blood pressure, too.

• **If your family is suffering, consider changing jobs.** No job is worth sacrificing your spouse or children. No career is more important than your relationship with those you love. Often, just considering a job change will alert you to other possibilities, such as moving to a home that's closer to work, thus saving hours in commuting each week. You could also take a half-hour lunch so you could leave work half an hour early.

• **Ask permission to work at home.** More and more companies are allowing employees to do this, especially if the job is computer-related. Find a Christian in the human resources department, and explain your desire to work at home in order to spend more time with your family.

• **Seek help from your personnel or employee relations department.** Family-oriented companies are seeing the need for in-house counseling when employees become overstressed.

Ultimately, it's in the employer's best interest to do something about overwork.

- **Negotiate with your boss.** Many superiors are simply unaware of the pressure they are putting on an employee's family by demanding overtime. Some believe that if an employee doesn't say anything, then everything's okay. Speak up! You may be surprised how reasonable your boss can be if you state your case.

The idolatry of work must be seen for what it is—a sustained and vicious attack on the family. Little wonder that a recent survey by Massachusetts Mutual Insurance found that Americans believe "parents having less time to spend with their families" is the single most important reason for the family's decline in our society.

As with most things, the modern world has turned divine values upside down. It's up to us—worker by worker—to get our lives and our families back on the right track.

Brian Knowles, who used to work 12-hour days, says he's down to 50 hours a week now. He works for a major insurance firm in Los Angeles.

15

Avoiding a Money Meltdown

Ron Blue

My daughter Cynthia called from college to say American Express had sent her an unsolicited application in the mail. The accompanying promotional material said that as a college student, she already had a good credit rating. Her question to me was, "Dad, don't I need to have a credit card to get a good credit rating?"

Due to my vocation, she has grown up in a home where money and money management are frequent topics of conversation. Yet even she didn't have a clear understanding of debt and credit.

It's true that most of the common uses of debt don't make much economic or biblical sense. However, something as simple as cashing a check usually requires two forms of identification, one of which needs to be a credit card. We live in a society that forces us to use credit or have good credit to transact the daily business of living.

The number of Americans who have absolutely zero debt throughout their lives is extremely small. Almost everyone has, or will have at some point, a home mortgage. In addition, every day you're confronted with the opportunity to borrow money for some purchase. It's essential, therefore, that you understand the different types of debt, the assumptions underlying them, and your own convictions to be able to respond wisely.

I also feel strongly that parents and grandparents should take the responsibility to train their children and grandchildren in the proper use of credit and debt. Children won't receive this training from anyone outside the home. It's not taught in schools or churches, and certainly not by peer groups. The home is the place where kids must get sound, consistent teaching.

Having credit cards does not cause one to go into debt. Not only do most of us have some debt and live in a society that compels us to have at least a working knowledge of credit and debt, but all of us, in the daily affairs of life, establish a credit record. Most of us seem to fear our credit rating, but it's really nothing to worry about when credit and debt are managed properly.

Credit Versus Debt

One of the primary points we need to understand is the difference between credit and debt. *Credit is having the right to borrow.* Credit deals with the potential borrower's integrity—his faithfulness and timeliness in paying his bills. Based on that integrity, a potential lender extends credit. That credit may require either the personal guarantee of the potential borrower, as with a "signature loan," or collateral—some type of security interest in something of value. This can be either the item purchased or another asset of the potential borrower.

Thus, credit is not the same thing as debt, but it is used to go into debt. Debt results when the credit extended is utilized for the purchase of some product or service. The Christian who believes having credit cards is wrong should understand that having credit cards does not cause one to go into debt. It only means credit has been made available to him. An individual's misuse of those credit cards causes him to go into debt.

It used to be that "being able to afford it" meant you could pay cash for whatever you were purchasing. If you didn't have the cash on hand, by definition you *couldn't* afford it. What a difference time makes! Today, "being able to afford it" has nothing to do with whether you have the resources to pay for it. It means strictly "being able to afford the monthly payments."

As such, every borrowing decision can be manipulated simply by extending the length of time of repayment in order to make it "affordable." Prior to World War II, home mortgages rarely went beyond 10 years. Today, 30 years is the standard, and in some cases, it's possible to get a 50-year mortgage. Fifty years may be longer than the home will last! But by extending the terms over half a century, the payments come down to the "affordable level."

This change in the way we view debt is one of its major deceptions. Debt-related deceptions are highly effective because they make borrowing appear to be the wise and logical thing to do. For example, if you believe that "being able to afford it" means being able to afford the payments rather than being able to pay cash, you're certainly not equipped to resist the advertising that offers "easy payments." Nor will you consistently resist the advertising slogan proclaiming "no interest for 90 days."

Credit Card Woes

A women's magazine tells the following tale:

Marcia never gave much thought to how much she was spending with credit cards. "My friends and I would go to the mall with our babies and spend the day just walking around," says the easy-going 33-year-old, who lives in a pleasant two-bedroom townhouse in a Chicago suburb.

"I was always buying things ahead of time: a cute outfit my son could wear next summer; a toy on sale that I could put away for Christmas. There was never anything major; just clothes, meals, gas, birthday gifts—I put them on my charge card. Truthfully, when I was charging I didn't feel like I was spending real cash."

Marcia takes off her designer glasses ("Charged, of course," she says, grinning) and continues. "My husband and I used to pay off our credit card bills completely each year with our income tax refund, so we had a great credit rating, and every year the banks would offer us a higher limit.

"Then, of course, there was the Sears card, Montgomery Ward, Lord & Taylor, Marshall Field, Lerner, Wiebolt, Amoco, Shell, Union 76. Oh, yeah, we also had a line of credit on our checking account for $2,000. It was great to know we could go out and get anything we needed anytime," adds Marcia.

Marcia and her husband, Ted, are hardly unusual. Today about seven out of 10 Americans use credit cards, totaling some 700 million accounts, according to the Federal Trade Commission.

There's no doubt these ubiquitous pieces of plastic are a tremendous convenience. They enable people to travel without a great deal of cash. They minimize the trauma of robberies (reporting the crime immediately means you won't be held responsible for the thief's bills). They make record-keeping easier, and they allow people to live more comfortably.

Financial counselors generally say one out of six people who buy on credit is burdened by excessive debt. And all the advantages of credit are easily outweighed by the headaches and heartaches that accompany a mounting stack of unpaid and unpayable bills (*Ladies' Home Journal*, April 1986).

Marcia and Ted's situation is a classic illustration of how easy it is to fall into the credit card trap. With more than 700 million credit card accounts for a total population of approximately 240 million, there are nearly three credit cards for every man, woman, and child in the United States. If you assume half the people don't have credit cards (because they're children), there are more than six credit cards per adult in America today.

Credit card companies aren't foolish, and they don't extend credit in order to lose money. What they've found is that merely putting a credit card in a potential user's hand will lead the person to spend 34 *percent more* than if the individual didn't use that credit card. And because their losses will typically run no more than 5 percent of the outstanding balances, lenders can afford the risk of putting credit into the hands of those who are not creditworthy. Charging an average of 14-18 percent interest, they much more than make up their losses from the millions of cardholders who pay their bills faithfully.

To determine whether you have a problem with debt, answer the following true-false questions (taken from Sian Ballen, *Money*, April 1987).

1. You spend the money in the expectation that your income will increase in the future.

2. You take cash advances on one credit card to pay off bills on another.

3. You spend more than 20 percent of your income on credit card bills.

4. You often fail to keep an accurate record of your purchases.

5. You have applied for more than five credit cards in the past 12 months.

6. You regularly pay for groceries with a credit card.

7. You often hide your credit card purchases from your family.

8. Owning several credit cards makes you feel richer.

9. You pay off your monthly credit bills but let others slide, such as doctors' bills and utility bills.

10. You like to collect cash from friends in restaurants and then charge the tab on your credit card.

11. You almost always make only the minimum payments rather than paying your entire credit card bill.

12. You have trouble imagining your life without credit.

Now score your responses. How many times did you answer true?

- 1-4 True. You can probably keep going. You don't splurge uncontrollably.
- 5-8 True. Slow down, you have entered the caution zone. It's time to draw up a budget, pay off your bills, and re-evaluate your spending habits.

• 9-12 True. You have to stop. You might be wise to consult a credit counselor or financial planner for help in changing your spending habits.

Misconceptions

People typically get into trouble with credit card debt because they fall victim to one or more popular misconceptions about credit. Their fall is hastened by the way these misconceptions appeal to our natural desires or fears, and by the fact that lenders aggressively promote this form of borrowing because they find it so profitable.

I'm going to cover four of the most common misunderstandings here. Three of them are ones with which people delude themselves, and one shows how subtly we can be misled by this form of credit.

1. You can't live without it. This easily accepted notion accounts for a lot of credit card purchases. To a large extent, it also accounts for why people who already have "enough" credit cards will apply for another when they see advertisements using that pitch.

Credit cards are used exclusively, however, to buy temporal and depreciating items—nothing of any permanence. They're often used to pay for entertainment, which is certainly important to living a well-rounded life. But it's not the reason for our existence. People also use them, as one wag put it, "to buy things they don't need with money they don't have to impress people they don't know."

One way to avoid unnecessary use of credit cards is to never make an impulse purchase. Always wait at least a day to buy something you want. If, after 24 hours and careful reflection, you still want the item enough to make a second trip back for it, you're more likely to be making a good decision.

2. Having a credit card means you're creditworthy. While credit card companies are concerned about creditworthiness, they're much more concerned about their profits. They're willing to take some significant losses while earning almost 20 percent in interest, plus the annual fees they charge.

Don't assume that just because you have a credit card, you can afford to take on debt. The test you took earlier should have highlighted for you whether you have a problem with credit cards. It's really scary, when you think about it, how easy it is to get approved on a credit card application. In some cases, it requires little more than your name, address, and telephone number.

3. You have to have a credit rating. A third misconception is that you have to have a credit rating or you need a credit rating. *There is no such thing as a credit rating.* Various organizations compile credit reports on people who have used credit, but there's no single source to which anyone could go to get your credit rating. There's no scale that evaluates you in relationship to everyone else.

Credit reporting agencies collect data regarding your credit history, payments, delinquencies, amounts borrowed, and so forth, but no central place gives you a credit rating.

The reality is that if you choose to avoid the use of credit cards, then even if there were a credit rating, you wouldn't need it. A credit rating presumes there's risk associated with lending you money. But if you never borrow money this way, there's no risk, and therefore no need for a credit rating.

Establishing a good credit history is simple. Pay all your bills on time, and establish some banking relationships: that is, maintain checking and savings accounts. You don't need to borrow in order to have a good credit report.

4. All interest is equal. Another misconception is that there's no difference between an interest rate and an interest charge, when in fact there's a big difference. For example, suppose you borrow $1,000 at 12 percent interest for one year, with the full amount due at the end of 12 months. At that point you would owe $1,120. The interest rate and the interest charge would be one and the same, 12 percent.

However, suppose you borrow the same $1,000 at 12 percent, but instead of paying it back with one payment at the end of the year, you pay it back at the rate of $93.33 ($1,120 divided by 12 months) per month. The stated interest charge is 12 percent, but the actual interest rate paid is now approximately 21 percent, even though the total of interest dollars paid remains the same in both cases ($120).

The reason is that as you pay the $93.33 each month, you reduce the amount of principal you still owe by about $83. Yet you're still paying 12 percent interest on the full $1,000 throughout the year, even though the principal shrinks steadily from month to month.

If you borrowed the $1,000 to buy a television set and a VCR, the salesperson would most likely tell you that was the "easy" way to pay for it. At only $93.33 per month, you could well "afford" it. But the fact is that while you could afford to take $93.33 plus interest out of your income each month, it was an extremely costly decision. Twenty-one percent interest, not many years ago, was considered usurious. Now it's considered normal for that type of purchase. This illustration graphically points out the deception of easy payments.

Years ago, the government required all lenders to disclose to the borrower what is known as the APR, a uniformly calculated annual percentage rate of interest. The proper way to evaluate what it costs to rent money is to know the APR—the real interest rate the lender has charged and you have paid.

There are many superficial differences between credit cards. They charge different fees and interest rates and have various ways of calculating the interest rate. They have different repayment terms, and many offer attractive "come-ons." For instance, I recently received a signed $500 check in the mail from a credit card company. I could cash the check, and the amount would be added to my credit card balance. I could then "repay the $500 conveniently over many months."

Other come-ons are free hotel rooms, frequent flier points, merchandise, and so forth, offered to induce you to either accept or use the credit card. Just remember, however, that credit grantors are not benevolent. The enticement will cost you something.

Recommendations

Most of us have to use credit cards at least occasionally to function within our credit card society. However, we don't have to use them to go into debt. There are three ways to get the benefits of using credit cards without going into debt:

1. Begin with a spending plan.
2. Use a debit card rather than a charge card.
3. Always pay the full balance at the end of the month.

My first recommendation is to begin with a spending plan. Unless you're operating according to that hated word, *budget*, you'll never have any real reason to control your spending. To use credit cards to fund your living expenses is to invite temptation into spending decisions. As stated earlier, researchers have shown that you'll spend 34 percent more using a credit card than if you don't.

The way to use credit cards legitimately is for convenience only, staying within your spending plan and paying the balance in full when the bill comes. If you haven't already done so, set up an annual spending plan.

My second recommendation is to use a debit card rather than a normal credit card. An amount charged to a debit card is immediately deducted from your bank or brokerage account balance. It's really no different from writing a check.

My wife and I have a card that lets us earn interest on the total account balance until either a charge comes in or a check written against the account clears the bank. When we use the debit card, we enter the item in our checkbook just as if we had written a check. Then we deduct it from our available balance. In place of the check number in the check register, we put "Visa." Using such a card allows you all the convenience advantages of a credit card, but you never have a credit card bill to pay because, in effect, it's paid the moment you use it.

My third recommendation is that for regular charge cards, never allow a month to go by without paying off the full balance. If you're tempted not to pay the full amount because it will make a big dent in your available cash, you're not using the credit card properly. A credit card can be a great convenience, but it should never be used to go into debt. The cost of credit card debt—12 to 21 percent interest—is always greater than the economic return of whatever the card was used to buy.

My final recommendation is that if you can't follow the above suggestions, or if the earlier test shows you have a problem with credit cards, destroy them. Make yourself a colorful decoration that can be hung on your refrigerator as a visual reminder of your problem and you'll never be tempted to use those cards again.

By the time the credit card companies send you unsolicited replacements, your spending patterns should be reset and the addiction to the use of credit cards broken.

Ron Blue is the founder and managing partner of Ronald Blue & Co., a financial advisory firm. He lives in the Atlanta area. This article is adapted from *Taming the Money Monster*. Published by Focus on the Family.

PART THREE

FOCUS ON WIVES AND MOTHERS

❧16

Women of Beauty and the Essence of Mystique

Jean Lush

"What do you do to lift yourself up out of the blues?" I asked a group of ladies in a support group I attended. We'd gathered that day to talk about overcoming depression.

"Oh, I go shopping," said Emily. "I try on all the lovely clothes I can't afford—minks, sequined dresses. Then I treat myself to lunch at Alexander's. The antiques and beautiful table settings and French waiters make me feel . . . elegant. I suppose it sounds silly, but I always go home feeling better."

"No," I said, "I don't think it's silly at all. You are surrounding yourself with beauty, and that makes you feel good. When I'm in a sore mood, I go out and pick or buy flowers. Then, as I arrange them and set them in their place, I admire them. I can almost feel the frustration or anger of depression flow out of me."

"I know what you mean," said Laura, one of the younger women. "I feel the same way when I go for a walk in the woods. I let my mind drift to all the beautiful things God made, and pretty soon I'm feeling at peace again."

Without even realizing it, these women recognize the human need for beauty. In my studies, I realized a fascinating truth. Women of mystique create beauty around them. They somehow recognize the tremendous human need for loveliness.

I think God knows how important beauty is to us. We have but to open our eyes to know He wanted us to be surrounded by beautiful things.

Days of Flower Arranging

During World War II, my husband and I lived in Australia. One of the block wardens, a friend of ours, told us an interesting story. He was concerned because people were resisting his instructional meetings on air raids, blackouts, and first aid. He said he'd finally chosen a day when he felt nearly everyone in the neighborhood would be free.

When he announced the meeting day, do you know what the women said? "Oh, no! That's the day I buy my flowers. That's my flower-arranging day."

With Japanese submarines in the bay and danger all around them, these women wouldn't give up their flower arranging. I'm sure they didn't consciously realize it, but in the midst of trouble, those flowers were basic to their well-being.

Think about how you feel when beauty surrounds you and when it doesn't. Imagine yourself sitting on the steps of a tenement house. You yawn with lazy despair. The ground is nearly bare, with an occasional clump of weeds cut to resemble grass. Garbage oozes over an open garbage can. You bend to pull one of the millions of weeds growing in the cracks of the walk that leads into the litter-lined street. Graffiti cover the fence. The words written in iridescent green make you turn away.

The housing development is only four years old, and already the paint is chipped and peeling on the once-white windowsills. Black soot covers the orange-red bricks. Your attention is brought back to the street as a passing truck driver hurls obscenities at a small child who crouches in the gutter to gather more stones. You wish you could wipe it all away, but it's too much . . . too hard.

Not a pretty sight. Lack of beauty—ugliness—brings grief to the spirit. Shabbiness and disorder drain us.

Now imagine the same place. A woman moves in next door. She scrubs and cleans inside and out, then sands and paints the trim a sparkling white. She waters the parched and patchy yard and scatters grass seed.

Maybe by now you feel a bit guilty and intrigued by the small but effective changes she's made. You ask if she'd mind if you worked together. She laughs and hands you a rake.

Together, you plant flowers and shrubs. You gather discarded bricks and create a garden full of forget-me-nots and candytufts. The child stops throwing rocks and comes to watch. You hand him a packet of seeds, and he smiles.

Can you feel the difference? Beauty creates energy. It lifts the spirit.

Inner Calm and Confidence

I did a survey a few years ago with 150 couples. I asked the men to list, in order, those things about their wives and home life that upset them the most. More men complained about bad housekeeping than about cooking, sex, or their wives' appearance. Men also have a need for a beautiful and tidy environment.

Contrary to what you may be thinking, it doesn't take a lot of money to create beauty. I have never been a woman of affluence. For some years during the Depression, we were quite poor. Yet my children recently told me they'd never realized it. I always set the dining room table with a linen cloth and china and nearly always arranged a centerpiece of fresh flowers on the table.

Perhaps because of my British upbringing, I stressed proper table manners. Even though we had little money, I tried to give my family a lovely environment whenever possible.

As for a woman of mystique, she has an inner calm and confidence. She loves herself and her body and portrays the essence of God, in whose image she was created.

This is perhaps the aura of mystery that is missing in so many women. A true woman of mystique has within her being a spiritual realm, filled with a loving God who gives her strength to cope with any situation.

She is constantly changing and growing. She is a mystery to men and women because she involves herself deeply in the things of God.

Her days are spent in learning God's ways and carrying out His will for her life through Bible study and prayer. She is in love with life, celebrating each moment, each day, as if it were her last. She is vital, growing, alive, and filled with the Spirit of God.

Our woman of mystique is by no means perfect. She is fully aware of her flaws and weaknesses, yet she is strong enough to admit them and not be embarrassed by them.

Perhaps a good illustration of a woman of mystique would be the virtuous woman in Proverbs 31. The woman acclaimed as a great wife and mother worked hard and was skilled in many areas. She managed her home and finances well. Her husband was proud of her, and her children called her blessed.

I know it sounds as though I've painted a picture of a woman who is impossible for us mere mortals to live up to. I offer all this information on mystique not to make you feel overwhelmed or guilty, but to help you grow. I know it looks unattainable, especially when you see all these virtuous attributes in one place. But I'd encourage you to go back to the beginning. Work on one thing at a time. Ask God to help you grow in the way He has chosen for you.

Possessing the qualities of the woman of mystique isn't going to magically transform your life. There are no assurances that even with mystique you'll have a devoted husband and happy-ever-after life. Nothing can guarantee that. But mystique can make you feel better about yourself, and make you a more appealing, more interesting, more exciting person to yourself and to others around you.

Jean Lush is a well-known speaker and author living in the Seattle area. This article is excerpted from *Emotional Phases of a Woman's Life*, ©1987 by Jean Lush and Patricia H. Rushford. Published by Fleming H. Revell, a division of Baker Book House Company. Used by permission.

❦17

Why Women Need Other Women

Ruth Senter

I was talking to a woman one day about friendship. "My husband is my best friend," she declared. "I don't need other friends." While I would not discredit or seek to invalidate her experience (in fact, I rejoiced with her in the strength of her marriage), I, for one, need women friends.

Today, my doorbell will ring, and a friend who works nearby will share her lunch break with me. We will eat sandwiches and catch up on the past two weeks since we've been together.

Last Saturday morning, a friend called from North Carolina to chat. "How are Mark and the kids?" she asked. "Any new writing projects?" And another close friend from my high school days recently dropped me a note. She was coming through Chicago on vacation with her family and wanted to get together.

129

Women friendships—long and meaningful relationships. Are they threats to my marriage or happy, comfortable additions?

Looking back on 27 years of marriage, I am struck by how much my friendships have enriched my relationship with my husband. Having close friends, for example, has meant that Mark—although he is my friend—doesn't need to be everything to me. I am less likely to try to squeeze from him all the emotional and spiritual reinforcement I need when I can draw upon other confidants as well.

An Example of Encouragement

Over lunch with a friend, for example, I can work through some of the disappointment I am feeling with the children. By the end of the day, when Mark comes home from his hour-long commute after teaching at the seminary, I have already been encouraged by my lunchtime acquaintance. I am able to listen to Mark talk about his day or walk around the yard with him and notice the growth of the Norway maple we just planted. There will be plenty of other days when I need Mark to listen to me.

Having close women friends also relieves Mark of the pressure to "always understand." He will not always understand. In fact, if he always understood, he would be a woman. The important thing is that there is someone who can look me in the eye and say, "I know, I've been there, too."

Last summer, my hands kept going to sleep at night, and my patience with our 14-year-old seemed at an all-time low. I had moments of emotional bleakness I'd never had before. Perhaps it was the home-decorating project I had undertaken for the summer. Maybe a bit of homesickness for our 17-year-old who was thousands of miles away, working at a missionary radio station for the summer. Mark had suggested I call Dr. Parker and schedule my annual physical a few months early.

In the meantime, I met my North Carolina friend at a weekend retreat. The first night, as we sat over a late-night cup of coffee, I felt as if I was hearing myself talk. Nelda was listing the exact symptoms I had described to Dr. Parker just five days earlier. We looked at each other and said the word together—"Menopause!" We laughed. She understood. How could Mark ever have known? I suddenly loved him even more for our differences.

Women friendships have also filled the holes for me when Mark has not been home. In our days of youth ministry, Mark was frequently away with the youth group, and we did not want to drag two preschoolers through the woods to a rugged camp somewhere. It was much easier to see Mark leave for the weekend when I would be taking the children and visiting a dear friend at her farm, just a short drive away.

Although there were times during those 12 years of youth ministry that I felt lonely and possessive of my husband, I have no doubt that I was less lonely because friends provided havens of warmth and happiness in Mark's absence. I have no doubt also that Mark felt freer to leave because he knew I would enjoy spending time with my friends.

His Idea of Relaxation

Mark and I were not far into our honeymoon when I learned that his idea of relaxation was not browsing through antique shops in quaint New Hampshire villages or looking for just the right gift in the country store at Old Sturbridge Village. He would rather be climbing Mount Washington or white-water rafting down the Swift River. Although there have been, and still are, times when Mark shops with me (and I go hiking with him), I am less prone to try and coax him into antique store expeditions when friends will gladly accompany me.

While I advocate women friendships, I am also the first to admit that establishing friendships has not been easy. Friends do not generally float into my life on a happy cloud of serendipity. I have had to pick up the phone and schedule a lunch, sit at my desk and write a note, or plan a day's outing to the city.

Maintaining a friendship also takes work. I have known the agony of having to admit to occasional insensitivity or negligence . . . to talking when I should have been listening . . . to comparing myself with my friend rather than giving her the praise she was due.

Another drawback is that I can only cultivate and sustain a limited number of close friendships. Careful thought and prayer are essential, lest I go rushing headlong into relationships that drain me rather than enrich my life. A friend should never become competition for my family.

If my husband and kids make statements like, "You're going out with her again this evening?" or "How many times have you talked to her on the phone today?" they may be feeling squeezed out by my friends. If so, I need to reconsider the relationship and attempt to restructure my involvement with that friend.

Friends, too, must understand my family priorities and must respect my husband and children. I know of a situation where a woman constantly cut down her friend's husband in his presence and behind his back. Fortunately, the friend was wise enough to confront the woman, and when the put-downs did not stop, she terminated the friendship.

While I am not overly jealous, I am on the alert if a friend always needs to touch my husband when she talks to him, if she carries on a conversation only with him when we're both present, or if she always calls to ask his advice. On the other hand, friendships that grow out of mutual respect have their own unique rewards.

Peggy and I have been friends since we were high school sopho-mores. Several months ago, she and I drove from Chicago to the Pennsylvania town of Manheim—the place where our friendship began. Her mother had died, and Peggy needed to go east to take care of business. So she invited me along for company. As we drove for 15 hours each way, we talked of where we've been, where we are today, and where we'd like to be 10 years from now. We laughed and cried together.

Nearing the end of the trip, the lights of the city were low on the horizon, and Peggy was asleep in the passenger seat as I drove. I had a sense of well-being, of continuity with my past and of anticipation for the future. Peggy had been part of my life for 30 years. She would be there tomorrow when I hopped into my car for the 30-minute ride to her house or when I picked up the phone to chat.

I almost laughed aloud as I thought of God's joyous grace. Peggy and I had gone our separate ways after high school. We both married ministers. Years and miles later, our husbands ended up teaching at the same seminary. To top it off, we both married men who like to go white-water rafting. And best of all, they like to do it together while their wives go shopping.

Ruth Senter lives near Chicago, and she has written many books.

18

How Women Can Stay Healthy

Dr. Joe McIlhaney

hroughout life, you will find it necessary to make decisions about your health. Sometimes these decisions will be matters of life and death. How will you make them? On what information will you base your choices?

Consider for a moment some of the decisions you may already have had to make: Are hysterectomies really necessary? Am I too old to have a baby? Is taking hormones after menopause a good idea?

These are just a few of the potentially life-changing decisions facing today's women, who go through four specific seasons: childhood, adolescence, the reproductive age, and menopause-postmenopause.

Although most women today have reasonably good knowledge of the structure of their bodies, there remains a great deal of interesting and helpful information that the average woman usually does not know about her own anatomy (structure) and physiology (function). Here are a few of the questions I'm most often asked:

What is included in an annual gynecological examination?

The routine examination varies from physician to physician, but the following guide suggests minimum expectations for the usual checkup.

Every year: An examination of the neck, breasts, abdomen, and pelvis; a blood pressure check; urine testing for sugar (diabetes) and infections of the kidneys or bladder; a Pap smear; and a weight check.

Beginning at age 40: In addition to the usual checks, these exams should include a mammogram every other year until age 50.

After age 50: A woman should have a mammogram every year from the age of 50 on. She should also have a proctoscopy (examination of the rectum and colon) or similar test.

What is PMS, or premenstrual syndrome?

PMS is the name used for a variety of physical and/or emotional problems that occur prior to a woman's menstrual period. Until just a few years ago, it was believed that PMS was an emotional problem rather than a physical one. Today, PMS is recognized as a medical problem and is treated as such by most physicians.

Symptoms of PMS may occur only one day a month or as long as two full weeks before the period starts. A woman may have only one symptom of PMS, such as heart palpitations or depression, or she may have many, including easy bruising, mouth ulcerations, paranoia, compulsive activity, food cravings, marital conflict, and even suicidal thoughts.

Because the onset of PMS seems to be associated with the production of progesterone at the time of ovulation, PMS can occur only during the time from ovulation until the menses begins (about 14 days). Problems that occur at other times during the month cannot be PMS. So, rather than using the diagnosis as an excuse to be irritable or sick, use it as a motivation to do all you can to control the problem.

The foundation treatment for PMS is limiting your intake of salt, sugar, and caffeine. Exercise can help. It is unlikely, however, that any drug alone will solve your PMS problem. Medications should be tried only after you make lifestyle changes.

Many PMS drugs can be purchased without a prescription at your local pharmacy. Most of them contain a mild diuretic for swelling, an antihistamine for tension and cramps, and acetaminophen for pain. If these work for you, there is no reason for you to see a physician for stronger medication.

If you have a major problem with PMS, a PMS clinic may be helpful. However, I recommend that you counsel first with your own physician.

Should I eat differently when I'm pregnant? How much weight should I gain during my pregnancy?

Actually, not enough is known about the nutritional requirements for pregnancy. A safe rule of thumb is to eat wholesome, healthy foods in amounts adequate to help your baby get the nutrition he or she needs.

During the last trimester, when the baby's brain cells are growing and dividing the fastest, a balanced diet is crucial to avoid permanently affecting the development of the brain.

Several years ago, women were advised to gain only 15 or 20 pounds during pregnancy, but this weight gain limit was literally "pulled out of the air." Experts now recommend a weight gain of between 25 and 35 pounds if the woman is of normal weight at the beginning of her pregnancy.

The reason for these new weight gain recommendations is that some pregnant women with diet restrictions during pregnancy were delivering babies with a lower birth weight and neurological damage.

Why are cesarean sections necessary?

Cesarean sections can prevent some ghastly ordeals for the pregnant mother and her baby. We tend to forget what labor and delivery were like when cesarean sections were not readily available. Formerly, a mother having an obstructed labor (because the baby was too large or her pelvic bones were too small for delivery) could stay in labor for days. The baby would often die in those circumstances.

Then forceps came into use, but they would often kill or maim the baby and could tear the mother's body, causing infection and bleeding.

Today, cesarean sections have contributed more to the health of babies and mothers than anything else in obstetrics. A baby too weak to tolerate labor can be delivered safely by cesarean section. If the placenta comes loose, a baby can be delivered before it detaches completely, thus saving a life. Likewise, if the placenta obstructs the uterine outlet, a C-section preserves the lives of both the mother and the child. C-sections have also decreased the number of babies born with cerebral palsy and physical damage from difficult deliveries.

Some potential danger lurks, however, in any surgery. Studies indicate that a mother has a slightly greater chance of dying from delivery with a cesarean section than if she has a vaginal delivery. Infections of the wound in the uterus, abdomen, or urinary tract are more likely with a cesarean section.

It is important that neither the doctor nor the mother feel that a cesarean section is an option to be taken lightly.

Should a woman take estrogen after menopause?

Yes, unless she has a major health problem such as liver disease, blood clots, a fibrocystic breast condition, or tumors that might be stimulated by estrogen.

There are several reasons a woman should take estrogen:

Decrease in osteoporosis. This thinning of the bones, which begins when the estrogen levels in some women's bodies start decreasing, makes the bones weaker and, thus, more susceptible to fractures.

Reduction of heart disease. Premenopausal women have a lower risk of heart attack than men of the same age, but postmenopausal women who do not take estrogen soon begin having heart attacks at the same rate as men. Recent studies show that if a woman will start taking estrogen immediately after menopause, she can lower by 50-75 percent her risk of having a stroke or a heart attack.

Relief of menopausal symptoms. If a woman is having annoying symptoms of inadequate hormones, such as headaches and depression, estrogen will relieve those symptoms and help her feel "normal" again.

Estrogen also helps keep the vagina from becoming dry and prevents the vaginal tissues from weakening. This helps decrease the possibility of hysterectomies and vaginal repairs later in life.

What is a Pap smear?

A Pap smear is a scraping of the surface of a woman's cervix or vagina with a brush or blunt wooden or plastic stick. The doctor transfers the scraping to a glass slide, adds a chemical fixative to the smear, and then sends it off to a pathologist.

The pathologist can usually determine if the cells have been inflamed by some infection or contains a premalignant or malignant growth. The surface cells of the body are continually sloughing off as new cells from underneath are growing. The cells that are sloughing off are picked up by the Pap smear. If a precancerous or cancerous growth is present, this area sloughs off cells at a much higher rate, perhaps 10 or 15 times as many cells as the normal tissue around it.

Why do I hear so much about breast cancer?

Breast cancer is a very serious malignancy and is, in fact, the number-two cancer killer of American women, striking one in nine. (Lung cancer is number one.) Survival rates of breast cancer patients depend on early detection.

Finding the cancer when it is small, even before it is large enough to feel, means it is less likely to have spread. For instance, if all women over 50 had mammograms every year, the death rate from breast cancer would drop by one-third.

Most mammogram machines expose a woman to less than one rad of X-ray, which is only about 0.1 percent of the level of radiation she receives from sunlight and natural radiation each year.

A mammogram is a simple procedure. Because it takes a moderate amount of pressure on the breast to obtain a good "picture," the procedure is a little painful. Try to tolerate the discomfort since the better the mammogram, the more likely it is to find a small growth in the breast.

What does "eating right" mean, and why is it so important?

The primary problem with the American diet is that during the past hundred years, we have started eating much more animal fat, fewer high-fiber carbohydrate foods (such as whole-grain bread and cereals), and more concentrated, non-nutritive sugar. The carbohydrate foods that we normally eat either have had most of their natural fiber content removed or they are "sugar carbohydrates," which are almost completely without fiber.

The human body was designed to function on a diet high in fiber and low in sugar, just as your new car engine was designed to run on gasoline high in octane and low in lead. If you run it on leaded gasoline, the engine will become gummed up and start functioning poorly. In the same way, your body will function poorly and deteriorate if you persist in eating the wrong diet.

It now seems that many of the common diseases and health problems we always thought were a natural part of growing older are due instead to the foods we have been eating. This is exciting news, because it means that if we establish new habits of eating, we can eliminate many of the diseases always assumed to be part of old age.

Dr. McIlhaney and his wife, Marion, have been married for 33 years and have three grown daughters. These questions and answers are excerpted from Dr. McIlhaney's book *1250 Health-Care Questions Women Ask*. Published by Focus on the Family.

*19

How to Manage PMS

Sharon Sneed, Ph.D. and Joe McIlhaney, M.D.

I (Sharon) spent many years not knowing why I had strange feelings at various times of the month. I spent sleepless nights wondering about intermittent aches and pains. I anguished over angry words spoken to a child, knowing I was temporarily out of control and overwhelmed with tension and irritability.

I am also a research scientist and have worked for years in a laboratory learning to be objective. From observing myself and other patients, I am convinced that premenstrual syndrome (PMS) is absolutely real.

As practicing clinicians who have helped numerous PMS patients, we firmly believe that treatment is crucial. And as Christians, we recognize treatment is also important for your spiritual life. So much anxiety and tension accompany PMS that many Christians equate its symptoms with a weakened relationship with God. We do not believe that is true.

We certainly don't have all the answers why PMS affects almost all women to some degree. We do, however, feel that diet, exercise, certain medical treatments—and prayer—can help women deal with it more positively.

Most physicians now agree that PMS is a real problem. A good definition has been written by Dr. K. Dalton: "A wide variety of regularly recurring physical and psychological symptoms which occur at the same time in the premenstrual period of each cycle."

Symptoms of PMS

Some of the following symptoms affect almost all women at some time, while others may be rare, even among PMS patients. Since so little is known about the syndrome, and the specific cause is undiscovered, this list is probably incomplete.

Physical Symptoms
- abdominal bloating
- generalized swelling of the body
- carpal tunnel syndrome (numbness of the hands related to swelling in the wrists)
- breast tenderness
- headaches
- skin rashes
- irritation of the eyes (conjunctivitis)
- backaches
- muscle spasms—pain in the arms and legs
- fatigue
- dizziness
- clumsiness
- heart palpitations
- increased problems with hypoglycemia

Emotional Symptoms
- tension
- irritability
- depression
- anxiety
- mood swings
- forgetfulness

- self-blaming
- desire to withdraw from people
- change in sexual interest (usually increases at the time of ovulation and decreases afterward)
- sleeping disorders
- inability to accomplish work at the usual pace
- indecisiveness (or the making of poor decisions)
- marital conflict
- increased appetite

In order to attribute any of these symptoms to PMS, they must occur only in the 14 days before—and at the start of—the menstrual period. You must be absolutely free of the symptoms as soon as your period is over.

If they occur at any other time, the culprit isn't PMS. Seek medical help for some other condition that may or may not be serious. Don't let PMS become a catchall diagnosis for your ailment.

Treatment Options

Many researchers and laypersons disagree about which treatments really work. Nonetheless, the treatment of PMS at specialized clinics and through private physicians is very similar.

Beware of so-called miracle promises. The miracle may be how quickly your wallet empties and how little your health improves.

Things You Can Do Yourself
- education
- pursue a regular exercise program
- maintain correct body weight
- choose a correct diet
    - PMS diet plan (for days when you have PMS symptoms)
    - Regular diet plan (for other days of the month)
- educate family and friends about PMS
- make lifestyle changes to accommodate PMS days
- control your stress

- take vitamin and mineral supplements

Treatment Requiring a Physician's Supervision
- correct diagnosis
- elimination of other medical problems
- referral to other professionals
  - for psychological help
  - for nutritional help
- prescription medications as needed
  - nonhormonal medications, such as diuretics and anti-anxiety preparations
  - hormonal therapy
- over-the-counter medications (get medical advice beforehand)

How Exercise Can Reduce PMS Symptoms

Every major publication about PMS that we researched included exercise as an important part of the program. Specifically, aerobic exercise was recommended. Some of the long-term benefits:

More energy. Tiredness is a common complaint of many women who suffer from PMS.

Greater productivity. The inability to make decisions and the presence of fatigue can dramatically lower productivity in school, the workplace, or home.

Decreased appetite. Increased appetite and various food cravings are very common symptoms of PMS.

Reduced stress. A moderate amount of stress in our lives is normal and healthy. However, if we are in poor physical condition, even a small amount of stress may feel excessive.

A more positive attitude. This may be attributed to endorphin secretion, which can accompany an aerobic exercise program. Some researchers feel PMS may be caused by the endorphin deficiencies that may occur premenstrually.

Improved ability to handle sugars. Exercise enables the body to handle sugar in a healthier way, with fewer peaks and valleys in the blood-sugar level. This can decrease hypoglycemic feelings.

Decreased body fat and improved weight maintenance.

Normalizing body-fat levels seems to normalize levels of certain hormones, which may improve PMS.

Diet and PMS

In a 1987 paper, Abraham and Rumley evaluated the clinical, bio-chemical, and endocrine effects of a total dietary program in patients with PMS. After PMS patients had kept to a healthier diet for three to six months, their symptoms improved noticeably.

Though three to six months is a long time to wait, your rewards will be long-lasting. Stay with it. Find new recipe books that make good-for-you foods also taste great. Think of this as a new lifetime atti-tude toward food—not something you do temporarily to make yourself feel better. You should practice good nutrition habits throughout the month, not just during the last seven to 10 days before your period. You probably should lose some weight, too. Being at your correct body weight will not only help you control PMS, but it will also improve your general health.

Premenstrual Dietary Guidelines

Avoid sugars. This includes table sugar, brown sugar, honey, molasses, jams, jellies, and sugary drinks. Hidden sugars are present in ketchup, sweet pickles and relish, many breakfast cereals, and sweet mustard. Avoiding sugar will help you control the hypoglycemic reactions that are common in some cases of PMS.

Avoid caffeine. Tea, coffee, many sodas, chocolate, and some aspirin-type preparations contain caffeine. Most PMS specialists agree that caffeine avoidance seems to reduce such symptoms as tension, anxiety, and insomnia.

Avoid salt excesses. Limit salty snacks, salty spices, and salty prepared foods. Beware of such condiments as soy sauce and Worcestershire sauce. Controlling your salt intake will help you control water retention and bloating during the premenstrual days.

Eat at least 1,200 calories per day. Hypoglycemic reactions—tiredness, fatigue, and lack of energy—may be worse if you severely restrict your calories.

Do not overeat. More specifically, do not consume too many high-fat, high-calorie foods during the premenstrual time. This can lead to lethargy and bloatedness.

Eat more frequently. Try eating five or six small meals during the days leading up to your period, rather than three traditional meals. Save something from each meal and eat it two hours later as a snack.

Avoid alcohol. Women are more sensitive to the effects of alcohol during their premenstrual phase.

Family and PMS

If you have a diagnosed case of PMS, you owe it to yourself to discuss it with your family. They will almost immediately realize the cyclical pattern of your irritability. They will also recognize that you do have good days—times when you are a different person. This will enable them to accept the "whole" you and even offer encouragement as you start your new PMS treatment program.

Lifestyle and PMS

What might normally be a slight problem may become a huge, anxious dilemma during PMS time. Carefully schedule your activities. Here are some practical ideas:

- Avoid demanding social commitments that require you to make elaborate preparations.
- Be more productive during other parts of your cycle so you'll have time to relax during PMS.
- Schedule vacations during the first two weeks after your period.
- If possible, arrange car pools and other such commitments on a rotation that frees you from responsibility when you are premenstrual.
- If you have young children at home, arrange for occasional baby-sitting during your menstrual time.

Prayer and PMS

All of life's situations need prayer, including PMS. During the PMS time, you may feel God doesn't hear your prayers and is far from you. In fact, He hears you and is close by. Prayer is a tremendous tool. Pray often and in faith.

Pray regularly. Be sure to continue your prayers and fellowship with God when you are premenstrual. This may seem unnatural at first, especially before the treatment program takes effect. Many women feel out of fellowship at this time and thus avoid prayer time. Don't fall into this trap.

Pray for the right physician. Pray that God will lead you to a physician who will meet your needs.

Pray for perseverance in your treatment program. Pray that God will give you the inner strength to continue indefinitely. This includes careful attention to diet and exercise.

Pray for your family and friends. Pray that with education and acceptance, your loved ones can come to understand this problem more clearly.

Excerpted from PMS: *What It Is and What You Can Do About It,* © 1988 by Sharon M. Sneed and Dr. Joe McIlhaney. Published by Baker Book House Company. Used by permission.

❧20

Ways for Moms to Make Money at Home

Cheri Fuller

W hen Pat Hawley's three children were small, she and her husband agreed it was important for her to stay home and care for the kids. Losing Pat's income, however, stretched the family's budget to the limit. Pat dreamed of having enough money to buy fabric to make the children's clothes.

The answer came when a friend asked her to make a bridesmaid's dress. After that successful venture, she began doing alterations and sewing for other friends.

At first, Pat worked 15 hours a week sewing clothes, but as business increased, so did her hours. She earned enough money to purchase a new sewing machine and start a college savings account for her children.

Today, Pat's children are grown and on their own, but the second income helps her and her husband take mission trips to construct churches in Mexico and Alaska. They can also afford to visit a daughter living in California.

Like Pat, I'm a mother who has a business at home. Our family's extra income comes from my free-lance writing. A typical weekday morning starts with fixing breakfast for my husband, Holmes, and our children, Alison and Chris. After waving good-bye, I throw a load of clothes in the washer, rinse the breakfast dishes, and run upstairs to my office.

I usually begin my business hours with phone calls to those I'm interviewing for magazine articles. After transcribing my tapes, I begin writing. The hours pass quickly.

As a home-based worker, life is never dull. I enjoy my work, but I'm still available for my husband and children—something I couldn't be when I was teaching full-time 10 years ago.

Back then, our oldest son, Justin (who's now in college), had just started junior high. The demands of my jobs—teaching and mothering—were simply too great. After Holmes and I prayed about it, we knew I had to give up the classroom.

I've never regretted that decision. With my new flexibility, I can watch Chris's 3:30 basketball games, pick Alison up from school, and be home when one of them is sick. I do have trying times when deadlines stack up like piles of laundry and it's my day to volunteer at school. But overall, I'm delighted with my arrangement.

A Growing Trend

Twenty-six million people—10 percent of the U.S. population—now work at least part-time in their home. No doubt some are white-collar professionals who, thanks to the growing availability of personal computers, fax machines, and modems, can work out of a spare bedroom.

But millions more are women who jumped off the career track to become mothers and raise a family. While some mothers start a home business as a creative outlet, many more moms work at home to bolster the family's income. A stay-at-home job bringing in a couple hundred dollars a month can often be the difference for young families struggling to make ends meet.

Last spring, I attended the first Oklahoma State Conference for Home-Based Businesses. Bright yellow-and-blue balloons were tied to the chairs, and in this festive environment, I was struck by the enthusiasm of hundreds of entrepreneurs.

That enthusiasm can be a part of your home. You should know at the offset, however, that a home business may not make much money when you're just starting out. At first, any profits will have to pay off materials and equipment. But as your home business grows, you should be able to earn enough money to pay for special family outings, unexpected medical bills, or the children's education.

Whatever your reason for beginning a home business, here are some tips to help you get a good start:

• **Assess your strengths and skills.** If you haven't already decided what to do, ask: *What do I enjoy most? What are my hobbies and interests?*

Be sure to consider volunteer work, as well as jobs you've held and skills you've acquired along the way. Barbara Brabec, author of *Homemade Money* and the newsletter *National Home Business Report*, says, "One passionate interest could be turned into a business."

For example, Cathy Bolton Adkinson's love of cooking led her to build a thriving home business that began with baking and selling chocolate chip cookies. That grew into cookie bouquets, cookie pizzas, her patented "cookie fries," and, ultimately, a gourmet bakery and cafe in Stillwater, Oklahoma.

Posy Baker Lough of Simsbury, Connecticut, grew up in a family that had money for gifts only if they made them. For Posy, this led to a home business that produces historic counted cross-stitch kits for museums, educational crafts and toys for children, and Advent and Lent calendars for families.

Before beginning a home business, you also need a clear understanding of yourself: Are you a self-starter? Do you enjoy working independently? Can you set up and follow your own schedules and deadlines? Are you organized and resourceful? How much money can you invest in this endeavor? Are your spouse and family supportive?

"Having the support of your family is important," says Cathy Adkinson. "My husband has iced cakes at 4:00 in the morning, babysat, and typed menus. It wouldn't have worked if he wasn't supportive. You can't have your spouse feeling bitter or resentful."

• **Learn all you can.** Successful home workers say that after defining their business interest, they went to the library and read about the field. It's also important to study the basics of running a small business. Be sure to read trade journals and magazines in your area of interest.

After Amy Webster had the idea for a line of greeting cards, "Blessed Are These," she spent three years learning the graphics business and how to draw children. She and her husband, Glen, went to home business seminars and checked out library books. They read all they could.

All that research paid off: The following year, her cards were displayed in 80 stores in the Southwest. A children's Scripture art book and calendar followed, and other new products are in the works.

• **Learn about your city's or county's legal and zoning requirements and tax guidelines.** Local chapters of the U.S. Small Business Administration can provide information, a free business start-up kit, and counseling services. Check also with the extension services of local universities. Many offer practical seminars on how to develop a business plan and keep tax records.

It's also important to check out the competition. Ask yourself: *Does anyone need my product or service? Where are my customers? How will I reach them? Can I make any money?*

"Be courageous and ask questions," says Amy Webster. "Ask a million of them, and learn from the answers. If you don't ask the questions, you won't find the open doors."

• **Don't be a sucker for get-rich-quick schemes.** Perhaps you've seen those tiny advertisements in the back of women's magazines: "Envelope stuffing. Make big bucks at home."

These come-ons usually ask you to send $15 "for more information," and what you get back is a letter detailing how you can set up a phony business like theirs. The U.S. Postal Service has clamped down on thousands of these fly-by-night operators. Remember: If it sounds too good to be true, it usually is.

• **Start small.** Sometimes in our enthusiasm for starting something new, we tend to get overextended financially. Keep your expenses low. If you're going to sell cosmetics out of your home, for instance, start with a small inventory. Keep supplies to a minimum, and scan the classified ads for second-hand office equipment.

You can save on advertising by sending out your own press releases; making brochures or flyers to put on community bulletin boards; spreading the word through friends and relatives with business cards; sending postcards to prospective customers; and finding other creative ways to let people know about your products or service.

Like most home businesses, Sherry Eden didn't have any money to advertise her gift basket business, "A Basket Case." So she started telling everyone she knew about her new venture. Sherry and her partner also sent invitations to "basket open houses" just before the holidays and the spring wedding season.

Soon, friends told friends, and the world was beating a path to Sherry's door. "Word of mouth has been our greatest advertising, and generating that interest has cost us very little," she says. One guest, a bakery owner, ordered 50 baskets, leading to a big account with a major corporation.

• **Network with others.** Because those of us who have home businesses can feel isolated, it's vital to "network" with others for moral support. We need to share problems, ideas, and encouragement. One way to do that is through newsletters, such as those mentioned in the resource list. You can also join small business and entrepreneur groups in your community.

Occasionally, I'll spend time with a few other writers over coffee to discuss projects and ideas. You never know when one idea will open the door to the next step your home business needs to take!

• **Manage your time and space.** As a home business mom, I try to get as much done as possible while the kids are in school. I also schedule my errands together so I'm not constantly running in and out.

Of course, if you're a mom with preschoolers, it will be difficult to set aside time—any amount of time—to work on a home business. Your first priority is your children. Perhaps you could work an hour or two while they nap or during a three-hour block one evening a week. You could trade baby-sitting with a friend or utilize the library story hour to do research, make lists, or outline plans.

On the other hand, if the kids are in school, ask yourself how much time you'll be able to work at your business. Set reasonable working hours, and try to keep them. Make "To Do" lists, but be flexible when your frozen pipes burst or a child is sick. An answering machine can help avoid interruptions during working hours.

Try to find your own niche at home where your materials or papers can be left at a moment's notice. If you have a spare room, that's great, but even a card table set up in your bedroom will work.

Judy Dungan, a Vienna, Virginia, mother of three, manages a congressman's fund raising, bill paying, and bookkeeping from her basement office, which also houses the children's playroom. "I worked there when my two- and three-year-olds napped. I appreciated being home with them, and now they are entertaining each other more so I can work while they play beside me," she says.

• **Involve your children in your work.** Some of the blessings of a home business include being there for first steps, impromptu trips to the park, and hearing the "hot-off-the-press" news when your children get home from school.

But how do we handle business and *still* spend time with our families? One seasoned home business mom advises, "Don't bite off more than you can chew!" That's especially true if you have toddlers or preschoolers. Remember: Children don't stay little forever. As they grow, so will your time for the business.

Some moms find creative ways to involve their children in work. My friend Melanie put two old typewriters in her office so her daughters could "compose" their own stories. You can fill a desk drawer in your office with crayons, paper, scissors, and paste so the kids can work alongside you on their own projects.

"One of the benefits of my home business has been the tremendous bond with our son, David," said Cathy Adkinson. "From the time he was two, he went on deliveries with me and made his own dough creations while I worked in the kitchen. David has really grown up with the business. As a result, he has great language skills and is fun to be with."

Kyser Lough earns money by helping Mom stamp and stuff envelopes in the "Posy Collection" mail-order business. As a preschooler, he went along on business errands. "We talked, sang, and learned in the car. We took side trips, got a balloon, and went to the park," says Posy. "I loved being available for him, and I still had an enjoyable outlet that provided extra money."

• **Be realistic.** Home workers, of course, save money on transportation, restaurant lunches, wardrobes, and child care. But a home business has its own unique difficulties and challenges. One of them is burnout. We wear many hats—designer, production worker, secretary, bookkeeper, file clerk, and even custodian. When you add taking care of children, it's a recipe for exhaustion.

"The number-one thing that can kill the business is burnout," says Amy Webster. "As home business people, we get weary. The business is three years down the road and doesn't seem to be any further along. We burn the midnight oil or get up at 5:00 A.M., working on a new idea.

"It helps to remember to be obedient to the Lord's leading, and keep your relationship to Him *first*. Listen to Him and do what He tells you, for it's one step at a time in a home business. If you're doing what God asks you, He'll strengthen you to do it, without sacrificing your family in the process."

IDEAS FOR HOME BUSINESSES

Family day care
Teaching cooking, music, or art (classes or one at a time)
Word processing and desktop publishing
Editing newsletters, free-lance writing, or technical writing for local businesses
Handcrafted toys, dolls, bears
Pottery, needlework, wreaths, ornaments, woodcrafts
Designing and producing jewelry, bows, headbands, T-shirts, and sweatshirts
Custom sewing, alterations, monogramming
Opening a bed-and-breakfast inn
Beauty consultant
Food: catering, specialty cookies, wedding and birthday cakes
Gift baskets
Gardening: fresh and dried herb products
Bookkeeping and accounting
Income tax preparation
Designing or refinishing furniture
Marketing: selling clothes or other products through sample sales or parties
Free-lance graphic artist

Where to Go for Help

Working at Home: The Dream That's Becoming a Trend
by Lindsey O'Connor
Harvest House, 1990

Home Sweet Home
P.O. Box 1254
Milton, WA 98354
   (Sample copies are $6 for a 100-page issue; $20 per year; quarterly)

HomeWork: A Home and Family Business Newsletter with a Christian Perspective
P.O. Box 2250
Gresham, OR 97030

Cooperative Extension Service
Oklahoma State University
209 Home Economics West
Stillwater, OK 74078-0337
   (Ask for a $4 resource that has information on defining the
   business, researching the market, legal requirements, pricing, and
   more.)

The Posy Collection: Christian Crafts for Families
Box 394
Simsbury, CT 06070

Cheri Fuller lives in Oklahoma City and is the author of several books.

21

Home Is Where the Business Is

Donna Partow

One of the most common questions people asked me during my pregnancy was, "Are you going to work after the baby arrives?" They were intrigued when I responded that yes, I was going to work, but I planned to do so from my home. Almost without exception, the women I talked with expressed strong interest in combining career and family, but they didn't know how to go about making that dream a reality.

Today when I talk to women about starting a home-based business, I frequently hear, "I couldn't possibly find the time." Yet many women spend 30 or 40 hours a week away from home and still manage to keep the household running smoothly. This objection points to an underlying fear that they wouldn't get anything done without a boss hovering over them or a production schedule driving them to meet deadlines. There's little doubt that your business will fail unless you learn to use your time wisely. Of course, working at home provides many distractions and temptations to get you off track. But how effectively you

155

use your time will largely determine how successful your business becomes.

Getting Started

One of the most important things you can do to help you with your decision about whether a home business is feasible for you is to do a time inventory. This will help you determine how much time you have for a home business and, once you've started it, can point out some areas where you can save time.

For one week, keep track of how you spend the better part of each half hour (TV, telephone, washing dishes, etc.). But don't suddenly spend two hours in prayer just to make yourself look good. Be honest, and try to follow your normal routine as much as possible.

If you're anything like me, this will serve as shock therapy! It may be disconcerting to realize how much of your time is spent on trivial pursuits. Still, the idea is to discern where your time is wasted so you can strive to recapture it. For me, time flies when I'm on the phone. Like many people, I have a tendency to continue talking long after the usefulness of the conversation has ceased.

If this is an area you struggle with, you may want to keep a close watch on your phone calls. It might be helpful to set your kitchen clock each time you pick up the phone or buy a telephone that electronically displays the time length of the conversation.

Conquering Time Wasters

As a self-employed business executive, you can no longer afford to allow time-wasters to control your life. The Bible commands us to "be very careful, then, how you live—not as unwise but as wise, making the most of every opportunity, because the days are evil" (Ephesians 5:15-16). The following tips may help:

• **Have a daily quiet time.** Ironically, one of the best ways to save time is to spend time. Each morning, set aside a quiet time of Scripture reading, reflection, and prayer. This investment will pay rich dividends throughout the day by giving you wisdom to deal with clients and make good decisions.

• **Learn to say no.** I realize many women, especially Christians, find this difficult. Somehow we have the idea that declining any request for our time and assistance is unspiritual. Nonsense! Jesus did not respond to every request while He walked the earth.

In fact, He channeled most of His time and energy into 12 men. Yet He was able to say, "I have brought you glory on earth by completing the work you gave me to do" (John 17:4). As Charles Hummel points out in his pamphlet *Tyranny of the Urgent*, Jesus was able to do so because "He discerned the Father's will day by day in a life of prayer. But this means He warded off the urgent and accomplished the important."

In the same manner, we need to be clear about our calling and purpose. Our top priority, of course, is our walk with the Lord. And for wives and mothers, the second priority must be providing and caring for both the physical and spiritual needs of our families. Be sure to keep first things first. Then, if you have time and energy to bake five dozen cookies for the church picnic, terrific. But don't feel you have to comply with every request that comes your way. That's a recipe for disaster.

• **Don't be a perfectionist.** When good enough is good enough, it's good enough. Is it absolutely necessary to spend two hours raking the backyard to remove every last leaf when the yard will be covered with leaves in an hour? Couldn't the dishes just drip-dry? Maybe I sound like a sloppy housewife, but the way I see it, life is too short to waste fussing over wax buildup.

Remember Parkinson's Law: Work expands to fill the time available for its completion. It even expands to fill time that's not available. Especially when it comes to housework, there's always more that could be done. I realize this is a matter of personal preference (and do take your family's viewpoint into consideration), but strive for balance in this area.

• **Stop procrastinating.** Again, Charles Hummel says it best: "Unanswered letters, unvisited friends, unwritten articles and unread books haunt quiet moments when we stop to evaluate." My most exhausting days are the ones in which I've accomplished the least, because frustration and regret sap all my strength.

If a job needs to be done, it's much better to tackle it and get it over with. Then you'll have the satisfaction of crossing it off your "To Do" list. If your business is going to succeed, you will have to exercise the "spirit . . . of self-discipline" (2 Timothy 1:7). That means pacing yourself to do a little each day rather than letting things get out of control before you take action.

• **Stop stewing.** Most would agree that too much of our precious energy is dissipated in bouts of worry, anger, and bitterness. Don't allow the difficulties of establishing a business to make you anxious. Worry is a waste of time. Pray about the obstacles you're facing, but don't worry about them (see Philippians 4:6-7).

Starting a business requires faith and trust in God's provision, so look at it as an opportunity to grow in these areas. If you find yourself getting discouraged, one of the wisest time investments you can make is memorizing Scripture to counteract negative thought patterns.

• **Stop shuffling papers.** Paper has a way of invading even the most well-ordered homes. Junk mail, magazines, newsletters, and the like are insidious time-wasters. Make it a rule to handle each piece of paper only once, if at all possible. Act on it, clip it, file it, or throw it away, but don't spend your time reshuffling the same old papers.

• **Schedule shopping trips for off-peak times.** Shopping for gifts the last weekend before Christmas is not wise, nor is grocery shopping on Saturday morning. This is particularly important if your business will involve shopping for supplies often. Also, keep those trips to a minimum by maintaining a list of things you need. Remember to buy in bulk.

• **Make the most of your waiting time.** Rather than reading the tabloid headlines while you're standing in line at the grocery store, pull out your "To Do" list and bring it up to date. Or you can meditate on Scripture passages, pray, or jot down any brilliant ideas that come to mind. Do the same while waiting at the dentist's office or bus stop. One of the best ways to use waiting time, and to manage your time in general, is to carry a personal notebook. Remember, your home business will be only as organized as you are.

Getting Organized

Is your house scattered with little slips of paper reminding you of things you're supposed to do or people you have to call? Or worse, is your head cluttered with thoughts such as, *What was I supposed to do today? What's the deadline for my project? What time does that meeting start?*

You can get rid of your jumbled thoughts and scattered notes by transferring everything into a personal notebook. As a home-based businesswoman, your personal and business lives are intricately intertwined.

A notebook will help balance and organize all the competing demands in your life.

Do important birthdays pass by without a call or card from you? Your friends will forgive you, but now that you're a businesswoman, such carelessness may cost you money. That's why the first section of your notebook should be your calendar. Here you will note important events, such as business appointments, deadlines, and meetings, as well as things you need to do.

Your notebook should also include an address section. This will come in handy as you seek to develop your business. For example, someone at church may mention that a cousin needs some typing done. You can jot down his name and number in the address section, then turn to your calendar and write "Call Susan's cousin, Bob Smith." Now that you have it in your notebook, you don't have to worry about forgetting it or misplacing the information. In fact, you don't even have to *think* about it anymore; your notebook will remind you.

Do you end up making several trips to the store to pick up things you forgot to put on your list the first time? Create a "Shopping List" section. Type up a list of all the things you usually buy each week, along with items that should always be in stock. You will probably want to make one list for food and household goods and another for business-related items. Make photocopies for your notebook. Then simply circle the items you need each week.

Setting Goals

By far, the most important section of any personal notebook should be entitled "Goals." I don't mean the resolutions you talk about on New Year's Eve and then forget by January 15. I'm talking about goals that stay with you throughout the year and affect the way you live each day. If you've never set any goals for yourself, now is the time to do so.

Even if it's not January (although that is the ideal time to establish goals), sit down with your notebook. Open to the first page of your "Goals" section, and begin to think and pray about what you want to accomplish with your life. These are your *lifetime goals* and may include things like "establish a successful home business" or "provide college tuition for the kids."

Finally, there are *daily goals*, which are the most specific of all. In other words, if your lifetime goal is to be a godly woman, and your yearly goal is to read through the Bible, you can do so by reading four or five pages per day. Most of the women I know think they could never find time to read the Bible in one year. It seems overwhelming, but don't you think you could read five pages in one day?

That's the advantage of breaking down your goals into manageable tasks: Things that looked impossible suddenly seem achievable. A time of reflection will help keep your priorities in focus and ensure that you attend to the important, not just the urgent.

Weekly Evaluation Worksheet

1. What did I study in my quiet times this week?
2. Which of my business and personal goals did I pursue?
3. Which of my goals did I fail to pursue?
4. Did I attend to the important or merely the urgent?
5. Am I using my unique gifts to develop my business?
6. Am I spending time in my office each day?
7. What specific goals do I have for the coming week?

Questions

- How and when did I waste time?
- What activities can be reduced, eliminated, or delegated?
- Did I attend to the truly important or merely urgent things in my life?
- Does my schedule reflect my priorities?
- Am I using my time to achieve the goals I've set for myself?
- Whom did I talk to on the phone? Were the calls important and necessary?
- Did some of the phone conversations continue beyond necessity? Could they have been shorter and still effective?
- Why do I want to start a home-based business?
- What has prevented me from getting started?
- What will be the most difficult part?

- Do I have any possible business ideas right now? If so, list them.
- Is there something I've always dreamed of doing? How can the dream become a reality through my home-based business?
- Do I think I'll have difficulty being my own boss and setting my own hours? Why or why not?
- How many hours per week do I plan to work? Write out a tentative schedule.

Donna Partow operates Syntax Service out of her home in Gilbert, Arizona, where she lives with her husband, Cameron, and their toddler, Leah. This material is taken from her book, *Homemade Business: A Woman's Step-By-Step Guide to Earning Money at Home.* Published by Focus on the Family.

22

Once-a-Month Cooking

Mimi Wilson and Mary Beth Lagerborg

O ne Saturday at lunchtime, John and his friend Chris were shooting baskets. John's mother, Nancy, invited Chris to stay for lunch. After serving the boys grilled cheese sandwiches, apple slices, potato chips, and glasses of milk, she returned to her chores.

Then Nancy overheard Chris say, "Wow, does your mom fix lunches like that all the time? My mom doesn't do lunches, and for dinner we pick a frozen dinner out of the freezer."

Chris was from a loving family, but cooking was not a high priority. Many mothers with busy schedules find the time-consuming task of preparing meals overwhelming. Instead, they're opting for fast foods, frozen dinners, and eating out more often than they would like.

All of us with growing children want them to eat nutritious meals. We want the family to enjoy their time together around the dinner table. We also want our meals to magically appear on time each evening.

We've found a way to do exactly that! If you've looked ahead in this chapter, you're probably wondering what a calendar menu, and a sample recipe are doing on these pages, so let us explain: We want to encourage you that you can conquer family dinnertime just as easily as we did. These are just a sampling of the several months' worth of menus, grocery lists, and step-by-step recipes we've organized for our book, *Once-a-Month Cooking*.

Some of you just read that book title and thought, *I can't think that far in advance. My life is already too busy!*

Trust us. This plan *will* help. Mimi began by cooking a week's worth of dinners one Saturday, then two and three weeks, and finally a month of meals in one day. She found that the plan saved time in the kitchen and grocery store, and it minimized food waste.

Moreover, it feels good to have meals on hand—ready to go. The woman of Proverbs 31 planned ahead: The oil for her lamps did not run out; her family was clothed against the cold; and she probably kept her maidens busy preparing food akin to the once-a-month cooking method. Since the Proverbs woman planned ahead, her time was freed for many other concerns, such as reaching out to the poor and needy.

This cooking plan also has allowed us to have a ministry to those who aren't able to cook. Using small, disposable dishes, we can freeze single or double portions for shut-ins or elderly relatives. Depending on the circumstance, we can either take the dish with preparation instructions or cook it and deliver it ready to serve. One friend cooks meals this way for her elderly parents when she visits them in another state. She then has the peace of mind of knowing they're eating well.

Not just women who work outside the home benefit. This plan is great for the young mother who cooks with a child on one hip and another hanging on her leg. Home-schooling moms have also used this plan to teach their children about food preparation and cooking measurements.

But what we like best of all is that after we've prepared a month or even two weeks of meals, we don't have to fall back on less-nutritious, quick-fix foods or the more costly restaurant meals. We're convinced the plan works and hope you will be, too.

Overview of the Plan

Before you get out the pots and pans and fix a batch of meals, here are a few hints to help you adapt once-a-month cooking to your lifestyle.

Remember that it's an easy system. For example, in the menu calendar on these pages, you'll notice seven different recipes requiring cooked chicken and five with a hamburger base. So, on your one cooking day, brown several pounds of hamburger while you're boiling or baking several chickens. Each entree is partially prepared or cooked and assembled in advance. Then they're put into sealed containers and stored in the freezer. When you're ready to serve a certain meal, all you have to do is thaw it, combine the ingredients, and cook the entree. And all that time-consuming preparation and cleanup is done at one time. (We hope you've noticed that on the first day of the menu—the one on which you cook all day—you treat yourself by planning to eat out that night.)

Second, as good as this plan sounds, you might protest, "I can't cook that way. I don't have a separate freezer."

You can store a month of meals in your refrigerator freezer by putting many of them in freezer bags instead of hard containers. At first you may not have room for three half-gallons of ice cream, two six-packs of juices, and three loaves of bread, but as you use the entrees, you can begin adding those food items. (Whether your freezer is large or small, cleaning it out before cooking day will be a big help.)

Food Preparation Guidelines

It also works best to shop one day and cook the next, because food preparation and cooking take a full day. (Some women prefer shopping one day, then spreading the preparation and cooking over two more days. Either way, expect to work hard for two full days.)

Some of the recipes call for bread dough, pastry shells, and pie crust, but we recommend you buy those from the store rather than make them yourself on cooking day. If you enjoy homemade pie crust, make it a couple of days ahead.

Finally, your day will go much better if you take a break to tend to the children's needs, make a phone call, or just sit down. Play uplifting music, and crack open a kitchen window for ventilation.

Grocery Shopping Hints

It may seem like a staggering expense to buy the amount of food required to prepare 30 dinner entrees. You may want to budget ahead and set aside extra funds. Even though it costs more in the beginning, you'll spend less over the course of a month because you'll be buying in bulk, eating out less often, and taking fewer trips to the supermarket.

Your shopping expedition is going to take a few hours, so make an outing of it. If you take young children along, be sure to go when everyone is well-fed and rested. It also helps to break up the trip. For example, go mid-morning to a discount food store or membership warehouse to buy in bulk. Then have lunch at your favorite place and finish any leftover shopping at the supermarket. If a friend baby-sits your kids on shopping day, you'll accomplish more in less time.

Money-Saving and Shopping Tips

You save the most money if you shop from a carefully prepared list. (Editor's note: Shopping lists for each month are included in the *Once-a-Month Cooking* book.) It takes superhuman strength, especially if your spouse and children are tagging along, not to toss a few impulse items into the basket. You've probably noticed that staple items such as meat, produce, dairy products, and bread are shelved along the sides and back walls of the store. To get to the necessities, you have to walk past tempting convenience foods such as chips, sodas, frozen dinners, and sugared cereals. Colorful cereal boxes with freebies are placed at children's eye-level so they'll pester you into buying them.

You can also save more money—and lots of time—when you make fewer trips to the store. Once you have your entrees in the freezer, you've done a major portion of your food preparation for the month. Of course, you'll still have to make those once-a-week trips for fresh produce, bread, milk, and eggs.

The Day Before Cooking Day

Ready to start cooking? First, clear off the kitchen counters, removing any appliances you won't be using. Then pull out your blender, food processor, mixer, and the bowls you'll need.

Make sure you have all the needed groceries on hand. If you don't have a food processor to chop and slice the vegetables, you may want to cut them up the day before cooking, since this is one of the most time-consuming tasks. Then store vegetables (except mushrooms) in cold water inside tightly sealed plastic containers, and place them in the refrigerator. You can omit the water if you put them in sealed, self-locking bags.

Finally, bring out the freezer containers you'll need. You may also want to have a quart jar on hand in case you want to save leftovers to make soup.

You can usually store the meals in freezer bags unless they're layered entrees like lasagna. Food stored in a freezer bag can be thawed in it and then warmed in a suitable container.

Setting Up an Assembly Order

The night before the cooking day, group your recipes that use similar ingredients, particularly meats.

Once you have your recipes in order, go through each one, tallying the total amount of each food item you'll need to process: how many cups of cheddar cheese to grate, carrots to shred, or ground beef to brown.

When you write out the assembly order, try to work with two or three recipes in the same category at a time, such as all the ground beef recipes or all the chicken. Record all the ingredients you'll need to store or freeze until the accompanying dishes are served.

Cooking Day

Think through the assembly order—the step-by-step outline of how to prepare all the entrees. (Editor's note: The book has all the steps.) Since you will usually be working on more than one recipe at a time, that will help you be better prepared and have a sense of how the steps flow together.

Place an empty trash can in the middle of the kitchen, and keep the pets elsewhere. You'll want to prevent wasted motion wherever possible on cooking day.

Use a timer to remind you that something is in the oven or boiling. Or use a notepad to jot down when an entree will be done.

Pause to wash pots and pans as necessary. Cleaning dishes and wiping up as you work will make your cleanup at the end of the day much easier.

If you have to sauté several food items in succession, use the same skillet. Often, all you have to do is wipe it out and put in the next ingredients. If you run out of stove burners, use an electric skillet or pan. It also helps to use a crockpot for stew or soup on cooking day.

Set frequently used spices along the back of the stove or a nearby counter. Use one set of measuring cups and spoons for wet ingredients and another for dry; that way, you'll need to wash them less often.

Perform all similar tasks at once. For example, do all the grating, chopping, and slicing of the carrots, celery, cheese, and onions at one time. Set them aside in separate bowls or plastic bags. Brown all the ground beef and sauté all the onions at once. Doing all those tasks may seem tedious, but you'll accomplish a lot. Assembling the dishes will go much faster.

At the end of your cooking day, use leftover sliced or diced vegetables and meats for a soup.

Let's get cooking!

RECIPE

Mexican Stroganoff
2 lbs round steak
2 teaspoons seasoned salt
1 cup finely chopped onion
1 teaspoon soy sauce
2 teaspoons minced garlic
1 8-oz can mushroom stems and pieces, drained
2 cloves
2 tablespoons vegetable oil
1 8-oz carton sour cream or low-fat yogurt
1/3 cup red wine vinegar
1 3/4 cups water
3 tablespoons all-purpose flour
1/2 cup chile sauce
1 12-oz pkg wide egg noodles
1 tablespoon paprika
1 tablespoon chili powder

Cut steak into bite-size pieces. Cook and stir steak, onion, and garlic in oil in a large saucepan over medium heat until brown. Drain off oil. Stir vinegar, water, chili sauce, paprika, chili powder, seasoned salt, soy sauce, and mushrooms into steak mixture. Bring to a boil; reduce heat. Cover and simmer one hour until meat is tender. Cool and store in freezer container.

To prepare for serving, thaw meat mixture and heat in saucepan until bubbly. Cook egg noodles according to package directions. Stir sour cream or low-fat yogurt and flour together; combine with stroganoff. Heat to a boil, stirring constantly. Reduce heat; simmer about one minute. Serve stroganoff over noodles. Makes six to eight servings.

Summary of processes: Cut steak in bite-size pieces; chop one cup onion; mince two cloves garlic.

Freeze in: six-cup container.

Serve with: Tomatoes stuffed with guacamole, corn on the cob.

❤❤❤

MENU CALENDAR

SUN.	MON.	TUES.	WED.	THURS.	FRI.	SAT.
	1 Eat Out— Cooking Day!	2 Split Pea Soup	3 Salad Bowl Puff	4 Jack Burgers	5 Deborah's Sweet and Sour Chicken	6 French Stew
7 Shish Kebabs	8 Chicken and Rice Pilaf	9 Grandma's Chili	10 Crustless Spinach Quiche	11 Grilled Ham Slices	12 Green Chili Enchiladas	13 Chicken a la King
14 Sausage and Rice	15 Oriental Chicken	16 Marinated Flank Steak	17 Saucy Hot Dogs	18 Currant Ham Loaf	19 Lasagna	20 Oven Barbecued Chicken & Cheesy Biscuits
21 Chicken Broccoli	22 Balkan Meatballs	23 Baked Beans & Hamburger	24 Jan's Sandwiches	25 Bird's Nest Pie	26 Chicken Tetrazzini	27 French Dip
28 Lemon Chicken	29 Grilled Fish	30 Mexican Stroganoff				

Mimi Wilson, her husband, Cal, and their children live in Ecuador, where they are missionaries. Mary Beth Lagerborg and her husband live near Denver.

23

A Woman's Guide to Financial Peace of Mind

Ron and Judy Blue

*F*inancial counselor Ron Blue and his wife, Judy, have teamed up in A Woman's Guide to Financial Peace of Mind *to encourage women that the world of money management doesn't have to be foreign territory. The material is based on their personal experiences as a family with three daughters and two sons, plus Ron's observations from his speaking and teaching, insights from 2,000 clients over the years, and the results of a nationwide survey conducted for this book by a group of Azusa Pacific University marketing students. The following is adapted from the Blues' book.*

Q. How do men and women differ in their financial decision making?

A. Women tend to be security-oriented in their attitude toward money, whereas men tend to be more motivated by a desire for significance. It's common, for example, for a husband to want to invest in the stock market while the wife wants to pay off the home mortgage. Men are driven more by the need to build something of significance than by the desire to provide short-term security for their families.

Q. Why do women need this information?

A. Many women have a lot of money management responsibility but little practical training. Women are also called on to communicate with their husbands in this vital area, but men may not feel comfortable discussing it. Husbands may think their wives won't understand the financial terms and concepts.

Like it or not, however, most women will end up managing all the household finances, since seven out of 10 married women become widows.

It's also been our observation that a mother is the primary trainer of children in managing money. Her role is probably the most significant influence they'll have. The value system she passes along is the one that children will take into their marriages and pass on to their own children.

The objective for our own daughters when they graduate from college and begin to manage their own income is the following:

- Tithe their gross income.
- Have no debt.
- Have a significant savings account.
- Manage their monthly expenses by a budget.
- Know how to manage a checking account.
- Know how to use credit cards responsibly.

Q. Do women have different financial needs at different stages in their lives?

A. Certainly. We've identified nine "seasons of life" that will influence a woman's specific needs. They are:

- The young single
- The young married
- The mother of young children
- The mother of teen and college-age children
- The empty-nest mother
- The retiree
- The widow

- The single mother
- The career single

A woman's relationship with her husband, be it good or bad, can also have a tremendous impact on her needs and views regarding money. (Imagine the outlook of the wife who told us, "My husband often seems unconcerned about his financial responsibility. I get the impression he really doesn't want to work.")

Q. But if we're trusting God, do we really need to be concerned about finances?

A. We recently received a letter from a woman who quoted numerous Scriptures that speak of God's provision for His people and of how we should trust in Him and not in riches. She said in part, "In light of these Scriptures and many others, should the church be reading (or writing) books that teach us how to handle our money so we can have a higher standard of living, save for retirement and vacations, and employ certain measures of risk to possibly increase our gains?"

She raises a legitimate question. Indeed, we should trust God. He is the source of all we have, and rather than worry, we can depend on Him to meet our needs. But that *doesn't* mean we shouldn't plan. We can see many cases in the Bible where planning was done with beneficial results.

When Joseph planned for the seven years of famine in Egypt by setting aside resources in the seven years of plenty, he was practicing sound financial planning. When Nehemiah rebuilt the walls of Jerusalem, he spent months in prayer, preparation, and planning before he even arrived at the city. The result: The walls were built in only 52 days.

David planned to provide the financial resources for his son Solomon to build the temple, and he collected them before his death. Jesus Himself, in urging people to count the cost of discipleship before committing themselves to His cause, referred to the wisdom of good financial planning: "Suppose one of you wants to build a tower. Will he not first sit down and estimate the cost to see if he has enough money to complete it? For if he lays the foundation and is not able to finish it, everyone who sees it will ridicule him, saying, 'This fellow began to build and was not able to finish'" (Luke 14:28-30). In Proverbs 15:22, we read, "Plans fail for lack of counsel, but with many advisers they succeed." That's an endorsement for good planning.

Q. Do we have to use a budget?

A. When the word *budget* is mentioned, almost invariably people think about constraints, inflexibility, rigidity, and guilt. In reality, however, a budget is just a short-term spending plan; preparing one simply means you decide ahead of time how you're going to spend your income.

Living with a budget is the same as taking a trip with a preplanned route—and that route leads to true freedom. The mere exercise of writing a budget will give you greater confidence in your financial situation than just about anything else you could do.

When you prepare a budget, priorities are set. The process helps you to avoid debt and to spot potential problems. It doesn't have to be an elaborate system, either. Elizabeth, a young single, told us how she controls her budget. She divides all her expenses into five categories and keeps one envelope in her purse for each. Her categories are:

- Overhead: rent and tithe.
- Loan payments: student loan and parent's loan.
- Food and fun: groceries and entertainment.
- Credit card charges for gasoline and travel.
- Utilities and phone.

Every month, she writes the amount she has budgeted onto each envelope. If she writes a check or uses a credit card, she records the amount on the envelope. If she pays cash, she puts the receipt inside it.

At the end of the month, she knows how much she has spent and can compare the amount to what she had budgeted. For the "Food and Fun" envelope that has actual cash in it, she stops spending when the envelope is empty. (That, incidentally, is the key to controlling a budget.)

Q. What's the best investment the average family can make?

A. Paying off all high-interest debt, including credit cards, car loans, and installment debts. That's the equivalent of investing with a return of 12 to 21 percent! Not even the most successful investors can achieve that rate of return year in and year out.

The question often comes up, "Should I take money out of savings to pay off that debt?" The answer is generally yes, because as soon as you stop *paying* interest, you can start *earning* it. However, don't leave yourself without money to cover emergencies (usually one to six months of living expenses). Pay off debt only with savings in excess of your emergency fund.

Q. What do you suggest for those shopping for a new car?

A. The first rule is always pay cash with the money you've saved. If you can afford to make monthly payments, you can afford to make monthly payments *ahead of time*—that is, *save* for a car. It may mean you drive your current car for a longer time before you purchase the new one, but it can be done. Research shows that the cheapest car you will ever drive is the one you own today. The cost of buying a new car or a recent model far outweighs the repair and maintenance costs of an older vehicle. It's never advantageous, from a purely economic standpoint, to replace your existing car.

We'd never recommend, however, that you drive an *unsafe* car. But an older car doesn't have to be mechanically unreliable or unsafe. Many people trade cars after just two or three years of ownership, so lots of safe cars are available at reduced prices.

Q. What are the biggest financial challenges in child rearing?

A. Training them in money management and the funding of a college education.

To learn how to manage money responsibly, children must have responsibility for managing money. They learn by doing. Our youngest son, 13, is a tennis player and has begun stringing rackets to pay for some of the extra costs of playing competitive tennis, such as expensive rackets. He's also saving to buy a car when he turns 16.

This has all been done with no argument, incentive, or inducement on our part. Rather, we gave him the responsibility, beginning at about age eight, of managing for himself the amounts we were willing to supply for clothes, spending money, lessons, and incidentals. He's seen that it's necessary to work to get some of the things he'd like. Therefore, it's been natural for him to save for long-term desires.

Children shouldn't leave home without knowing how to manage money, balance a checkbook, use a credit card responsibly, and set up a simple budget. A caution here: One of the greatest problems is the differences in the parents' and children's expectations. Children may expect, for example, to buy Polo shirts, have new cars when they reach 16, have college totally paid for, get help from Mom and Dad in acquiring their first home, and so on.

Parents, on the other hand, may have no intention of providing all those expectations. You need to make your decisions early about what you'll provide in the way of cars, college, first homes, and wedding expenses. By communicating your decisions early, your children will have time to accept the reality.

Q. Any closing advice?

A. Just that you shouldn't expect to achieve financial freedom or peace of mind immediately. Just take the first step God has impressed upon you now. The second step, whatever it may be, will become apparent after the first has been taken.

God never seems to reveal His entire plan ahead of time. What He does reveal is the next step. Abraham was told to sacrifice his son Isaac. He didn't know a ram would be provided. All he knew was that he had been given an order, and he was to faithfully carry it out.

In the parable of the talents in Matthew 25, Jesus told of the servant who heard his master say, "Well done, good and faithful servant! You have been faithful with a few things; I will put you in charge of many things. Come and share your master's happiness!" (verse 21).

Our desire is that you stand before the Lord one day and hear Him utter those words. We want that for ourselves as well.

Ron and Judy Blue have been married for 28 years.

PART FOUR

FOCUS ON DIFFICULT FAMILY PROBLEMS

🌱24

Married, No Children

Becky Foster Still

"**A**unt Becky, why aren't you a mommy?"

The frank question, posed so innocently by my curious five-year-old niece at a family gathering last year, sent an instant, familiar stab of pain straight to my heart. Looking down at the little girl's expectant face, I inwardly prayed that my reply would close the subject: "God just hasn't blessed your Uncle Mike and me with any little ones yet, sweetheart."

At that time, more than two years had passed since my husband and I first started "trying" for a pregnancy. I should have been used to questions like my young niece's—but I wasn't. And not only children, but well-meaning friends and family members sometimes offered comments or questions that stung: "So when can we expect a great-grandchild?" "Loosen up! You two just need to relax, and it will happen." "Has Mike switched to boxer shorts yet?"

The ability to have children is something most of us take for granted as we grow up, marry, and make plans to start a family. One couple out of every six, however, discover that a fertility problem means childbearing is not so easy for them.

A couple is generally said to be *infertile* when they have tried unsuccessfully to conceive for one year or longer. The term should never be confused with *sterility*, which is a permanent condition. Many infertile couples eventually do bear children with medical help or just with time; others do not and decide to adopt or live without children in the family.

Infertility is an increasingly common problem today, largely because many are waiting to have children later in life. Conditions that impair infertility are most often hereditary in origin—but can arise or worsen with age.

The cause of fertility impairment is equally likely to lie with *either* husband or wife. Many times, as in my marriage, a combination of factors in both partners affects the ability to bear children. And for some childless couples, a medical explanation is never determined with certainty.

Endless Frustration

Infertility is a private subject, one that few of us are comfortable talking about. Yet the anxiety the infertile couple feels is very real, and the "under-wraps" nature of the problem often serves to compound their pain. Those who desire children have no tangible loss to mourn; there are few socially acceptable ways for them to vent their emotions of sorrow and frustration. And their fertile friends—parents who might be absorbed themselves in the challenges of child raising—sometimes find it hard to fully empathize.

The frustrations of infertility can seem endless. Not only are many of the medical procedures expensive, but frequent trips to the doctor's office are time-consuming and stressful. For my husband and me, every visit was a scheduled reminder of our "problem." Many doctors who treat infertility are obstetrician/gynecologists who also deliver babies. I can recall many a miserable moment spent in waiting rooms filled with glowing, pregnant women.

In the darkest hours, it seems to the infertile husband and wife that God is not being fair. It was hard for me to hear about a "surprise pregnancy" from friends who had already been blessed with several children. *Why them, Lord, and not us?* Childless couples usually feel strongly that they would be good parents—yet we all see the media saturated with accounts of child abuse and abortion. *Don't we deserve a pregnancy more than they do, Lord?*

Those who truly desire a child will usually do whatever they can to improve their chances: taking the wife's temperature every morning, discussing intimate details with their doctor, scheduling sex on the calendar, and abstaining when ordered. Sometimes it seems as if a medical team has been invited into the bedroom. At first, Mike and I joked about the "prescription" we were given that detailed when and how we were to be intimate with each other. It didn't take long, though, for the humor to wear off.

Such a loss of spontaneity and privacy inevitably causes strain between husband and wife. And other concerns surface, too. When an actual medical condition is found, the "responsible" partner often experiences guilt—and the other spouse might destructively cast blame. Or the husband and wife may not agree on the extent to which medical treatment should be pursued. A friend of mine, for example, would like to consider surgery that could potentially correct their problem, but her husband prefers to "let nature take its course."

Mike and I were fortunate: The infertility experience bonded us closer together. For many others, though, the ordeal can create tension and conflict that gnaw away at the relationship.

The Goal of Motherhood

Although there are exceptions, women tend to face a greater emotional struggle with infertility than do men. Many women, especially those raised in Christian homes, develop a sense of identity that is closely linked with motherhood. Little girls look forward to someday bearing and nurturing their own children, and those dreams are strongly reinforced up through adulthood. Even if she becomes committed to a career, a woman will still hold motherhood as a deeply cherished part of her plans.

Little boys, by contrast, don't give a lot of thought to fatherhood as they grow up. For the Christian man, being a parent is important—and for many it does become their primary goal—but a man is just as likely to also find identity in his occupation or other interests.

Women, too, encounter reminders of their childless state more frequently than their husbands do. Traditional women's magazines target mothers with a house full of toddlers or teenagers. Other people usually see the wife as the one who is responsible for "family" matters. Outsiders almost always ask me, not Mike, whether we have any children in our family.

And in social situations among married women, conversation often turns to family, children, babies, and pregnancies. A woman I used to work with, expecting her second child, took to confiding in me daily about her insatiable cravings and ever-expanding waistline. Secretly I wished she would feel as free to discuss these details with Frank, our friendly co-worker across the hall, instead of me!

Because infertility can threaten a woman's firmly ingrained hopes, dreams, and very self-image, women often feel the pain of infertility quite deeply—more than even their husbands recognize. It is extremely common for the infertile woman to be envious or even resentful of others who are blessed with easy fertility. For those who are struggling, it can be tough to act overjoyed at the news of a friend's pregnancy! And the Christian woman, in particular, may have trouble accepting such negative emotions in herself—so she will often bottle them up, leading to more stress.

The mini-"baby boom" that is now sweeping our continent can rub salt in the wound, too. Babies and pregnant women are everywhere—in the mall, on the bus, at work—and you can be sure that infertile women notice every one of them. Most, as they come to terms with their infertility, eventually become less sensitive to such things. But for some women, unfortunately, the longing to have children of their own develops into an obsession, dominating their thoughts constantly.

As my husband and I have worked through our own fertility struggles, we have discovered how significant a role friends and family can play by providing us with needed emotional support. Infertility being such a delicate subject, though, many don't know what to say to the childless couple they care about. Having listened to other infertile husbands and wives voice the same feelings, frustrations, and experiences we have confronted, I now understand there are things others can do to help their friends weather the infertility process.

Be informed.

• With more and more couples facing infertility today, you may not realize how many of the people you know are encountering the problem. Don't joke about the subject— your comments might hit a sour note for someone listening to you.

• Infertility affects couples, not individuals. Don't think in terms of the problem being either partner's "fault."

• Remember that infertility is not a lifelong condition for many. According to Dr. Joe S. McIlhaney, a noted Christian infertility specialist in Austin, Texas, at least 50 percent of those who seek infertility treatment will eventually conceive—and, because of improving medical techniques, this success rate is increasing.

• Causes are most often hereditary in nature. Such conditions as sexually transmitted disease or prior abortion can lead to infertility, but in the vast majority of cases, a couple did nothing "wrong" to bring about their problems.

• Recognize that your childless friends might be under financial stress. Many assume that since these couples don't have children, their bank accounts must be healthy. Fertility treatments, however, can be very expensive— corrective surgery, for example, can total $8,000 or more—and health insurance does not necessarily cover all the costs.

• Be aware of the expenses and stress involved in adoption, too. Today, a couple can expect to pay anywhere from $2,000 to $20,000 for an adoption, and it is common to wait at least two years for a baby.

Be sensitive at holiday times and other special occasions.

• Know that Mother's Day can be one of the hardest days of the year for the woman who wants to be a mother but isn't. Going to church can be rough, because this Sunday service tends to focus attention on the institution of motherhood, honoring the mothers in the congregation. Make it a point to spend some extra time with a childless friend on Mother's Day—even if it's just to call her up or pull her aside at church and chat for a bit.

• Other holidays, too, center on children—Christmas and Easter, for example—and can be difficult for the infertile couple. Growing up, many of us fantasized about how we would celebrate holidays with our children and carry on family traditions. But for those who still have no young ones in the home, holiday times can seem hollow, with festivities bringing painful reminders of their frustration.

Holiday family gatherings also provide the perfect scenario for curious relatives to ask insensitive questions. Aunt Mabel doesn't hesitate to ask what the baby hold-up is—and to offer unsolicited advice. In large family gatherings, too, joyful announcements of other pregnancies and new babies are common. Be sensitive to your childless sister's feelings at these times, and understand if, on occasion, she and her husband decide not to attend the family get-together.

Be a good listener.

• Don't offer advice unless it's asked for. If a couple are trying to have a child, they are almost certainly well aware already of the steps that can be taken to improve fertility.

• Tread lightly when it comes to discussing a friend's infertility. Take your cues from him or her. Broach the subject only if your friend has already told you she has a fertility problem, and only if she seems to want to talk about it. Offer to be there for her, to pray with her if she wants to, but don't push. She may feel more like opening up with you at a later time.

Don't assume that men don't hurt.

• Women may generally have a harder time with infertility, but every individual is different. Men can hurt deeply, too. For many men, infertility represents a threat to their sense of masculinity. Be sensitive to the husband—and remember that this is by no means a "woman's problem" only.

Treat the infertile friend just as you would any good friend.

• Don't pity your infertile friend, be overly solicitous, or treat him differently from any other friend. Your friend may have already come to terms with this condition in his life; infertility is a process during which feelings and levels of acceptance evolve. And individuals cope differently— having a biological child, for some, is not a major goal in life. Just try to know your friend well.

Above all, remember the wisdom of Proverbs 17:17: "A friend loves at all times." Be a good friend . . . and a sensitive one. Know that infertility can cause great emotional strain and that many conceal their stress well.

If you suspect a friend is struggling with this problem, think of the little things you can do. When you sense your friend's mood is low, call on the telephone for a chat. Or send a note that just says "Hi." Pray for your friend. Show the infertile couple your Christian love—with actions more than with words!

Since writing this story, Becky Still gave birth to a daughter. She and her family live in Southern California.

25

Adoption: The Possible Dream

Melanie Hemry

*P*eople in the hospital waiting room began to stare. Was it my pacing and the incessant clicking of my heels against the tile floor? Or the half-sick, almost hopeful looks my husband, Ken, and I gave one another?

I had become an expert at waiting.

"Just relax!" my friend Mildred told me when I didn't get pregnant the first year we tried to start a family. I wished the problem were that simple. Uptight teenagers get pregnant in the backseats of cars. Yet dozens of well-meaning friends told me to relax.

I relaxed through tests and exams. I relaxed through a series of infertility drugs. I was not relaxed when I opted for surgery—I was desperate.

But none of the doctors had the medical magic I needed. The day came when I had to face reality. Nothing more could be done.

I grieved—for the children I never would carry, for the all-too-quiet house, and for those first steps we'd never see. I grieved for the first lost tooth that would never go under a pillow and the first set of car keys we'd never hand over. I grieved for an auburn-haired child with Ken's laughing eyes.

Ultimately, I decided the loss was too great. My dream of a family was too deep. I couldn't let go. Ken and I discussed adoption, but we heard the wait could take years.

I called the director of a local adoption agency. "I'm sorry," he said. "Since your husband is seven years older than you, your average age is over 35. You don't fit our profile for adoptive parents." *They won't even send us an application!* Had I waited all this time to be told I was too *old* to be a mother? Every agency we contacted told us the same thing. We had waited too long.

Ken discovered that our state, Oklahoma, allows independent placement (also known as private adoption). We sent letters and pictures of ourselves to doctors and lawyers around the state. We knew we were swimming against the tide. Less than 7 percent of unwed teenagers place their babies for adoption. Around half abort, and the rest become single parents.

Those who choose to carry their babies to term often hear that adoption is "giving away their flesh and blood" rather than a self- sacrificing way to provide a good home for a child they love.

Ken and I desperately *wanted* to provide that good home. As months turned to years, we continued to turn to the Lord in prayer.

It finally happened. A young, unmarried woman wanted a couple just like us to adopt her child. We fit her profile! We were told all about her, and she about us. I ironed the ruffles on the bassinet and set toys on the nursery shelves. Then the news came. The baby was a boy.

He was stillborn.

There were days when we didn't think we'd ever get over our grief. The loss seemed to wash over us in waves. As a registered nurse working in the intensive care unit, I'd faced difficult situations. But taking down that bassinet was the hardest thing I'd ever done. Something in me was dying. Maybe it was hope.

But now, as I paced the waiting room, a woman I had never met was standing before a downtown judge. She'd already made the courageous decision to give her child life. Now, she was renewing mine.

"Mr. and Mrs. Hemry?" the hospital administrator called, leading us to his office. Moments later, Heather Elise Hemry was placed in my arms, filling the aching loss of an 11-year wait.

Long Odds

Somehow, Ken and I were among the 25,000 parents who beat the odds and adopted an infant that year. Estimates of the number of prospective parents waiting to adopt range from a low of one million to over two million. Yet only 51,000 unrelated domestic adoptions (25,000 were infants) and 10,000 international adoptions took place in 1986, for example.

So, how *can* you beat the odds and adopt? Start at the top. Psalm 68:5-6 says it is God who is Father to the fatherless, and He places the solitary into families.

The first step to successful adoption is prayer.

The next step is to determine your adoption options. They are:

• **Agency adoption.** The birth mother makes an adoption plan with an agency of her choice, entrusting them to handle the legalities and place her child in a loving home.

Adoption agencies vary in size and services from small church-supported ministries to large organizations. These private agencies usually offer counseling for the birth mother as well as the adoptive parents, who may still need assistance in dealing with the grief of infertility.

In addition, agencies like the Edna Gladney Center in Fort Worth, Texas, provide living accommodations and an on-site hospital for the birth mother. Gladney is the only center to offer middle and high schools on the grounds. For the birth mother who has completed high school, they have a career development center offering classes on a variety of subjects.

Adoption is also available through the Department of Children's Services in each state. These state services are known as public agencies and are generally the least expensive way to adopt.

Whether adopting through a public or private agency, prospective parents should understand that after birth, the baby will be placed in foster care until the waiting period for the birth mother to change her mind has passed. This protects the adoptive parents from the emotional trauma of bonding to a child they may not be able to adopt.

• **Independent placement.** In independent placement (also known as private adoption), the birth mother makes an adoption plan with a lawyer. She either chooses the adoptive parents herself or selects them from profiles of prospective parents. Counseling services are not generally provided in independent placement, although the birth mother and adoptive parents are sometimes counseled by their minister or other local clergy.

State laws allow independent placement in 44 states. Although statutes vary, the adoptive parents generally must pay attorney's fees, court costs, the birth mother's medical bills, and, in some cases, part of the birth mother's living expenses until the child is born.

Parents adopting through independent placement may still use foster care during the waiting period, as is done in agency adoption, or bring the baby directly home from the hospital. Most skip the foster care, believing it is in the child's best interest, emotionally, not to be placed in a transition home during the bonding period.

• **Unidentified vs. open adoption.** Whether adopting through an agency or independent placement, couples may go the traditional route or have an open adoption. The first is confidential, shielding the identities of birth mother and adoptive parents while still exchanging necessary medical and vocational histories.

The second lets the birth mother and adoptive parents openly know one another. They often meet before the birth of the child and continue a relationship afterward. Many adoption experts are wary of these relationships, and they should be prayerfully considered. Ann Kiemel Anderson's book *Open Adoption: My Story of Love and Laughter* may help anyone considering this type of adoption.

Getting a Start

How does one start the adoption process? Attorney Jack Petty, director of Bethany Adoption Services in Bethany, Oklahoma, says, "First, contact all the local adoption agencies in your area to see if you fit their parent profile. Ask how many placements they've made, whether they require money up front, and if they have a pre-qualification application.

"Don't limit yourselves to the large state or national agencies. You may get more attention through local church-supported or small denominational agencies. I have a high level of trust for these agencies, though they are less known."

The next step is to find an attorney with experience in local and Interstate Compact adoption. The Interstate Compact on the Placement of Children (ICPC) states that no child can be sent across state lines without first getting approval from the Interstate Compact office in *both* states. "Ask for attorney recommendations from adoption agencies, your state's certified specialist in adoption, a local judge, the welfare office, or the state bar association," says Petty. "Another way is to go to the courthouse and find out which lawyer handles the most adoptions."

Petty estimates the average waiting period is 15 months to two years. "Couples seeking to adopt are often almost afraid to talk about the process," Petty explains. "They often keep their plans to themselves. Unfortunately, that is the worst thing to do.

"I've noticed that the parents who have adopted strengthened their own odds by networking. They took charge of the process as much as they could by spreading the word they wanted to adopt. They joined parent support groups. I can't stress how important this is. People who have already adopted are the best resource you have."

Another successful strategy is gaining the support of physicians, pastors, and other professionals in your community. These people may be counseling a birth mother who has an adoption plan and is searching for someone to parent the child.

From Faraway Lands

More and more couples look beyond our borders to adopt. Linda Hicks and her husband, Alan, adopted a Korean girl through Dillon International in Tulsa, Oklahoma. "We didn't even apply for a domestic adoption," Linda recalls. "We knew from the beginning that we wanted to adopt internationally. I remember the day Alan and I first got to read about Caroline," says Linda. "We both had a set of papers with a picture on the last page. We were careful to turn each page at the same time so neither of us would see the picture first. When we were ready for the last page, we turned at the same instant—and burst into tears. Bonding with an adoptive child often takes time, but we bonded with Caroline the moment we saw that picture. I couldn't love her more deeply."

Kay Moore, from Jacksonville, Texas, flew to Honduras in 1987 with a representative of the Texas Baptist Home for Children. In the

Central American country, she got her first look at Joshua, the infant she and her husband, David, hoped to adopt. While the missionary who usually cared for Joshua was in the United States, Kay, unable to speak Spanish, stayed at the mission for six weeks and cared for Joshua. Six months later, David and Kay flew back to Honduras to finalize the adoption and bring Joshua home.

Kay and David are among the many couples who adopt from countries requiring the parents to travel there. "The plane trips were expensive," Kay admits, "but there is something about seeing your child's birthplace that gives you a deep respect for his roots." Later, the Moores traveled once again to Honduras to adopt their daughter, Jolisa.

While domestic and international adoptions of infants compose a large part of the children adopted each year, an estimated 36,000 children of the 300,000 in foster care are ready to be adopted. Many of the waiting children are classified as "special needs"—sibling groups who need a home together, minorities, older children, or those with emotional or physical difficulties.

Looking through the photo books of children waiting to be adopted is a good way to get an idea of what would be involved in adopting a special-needs child. Many couples, having heard that "special needs" means severely disabled, dismiss this option too quickly. Some children merely had the misfortune of entering the system a year or two past the "cute" stage.

An Answer to Prayer

One family who beat the adoption odds are our friends, Vic and Robin Porter. "We'd tried to get pregnant or adopt for seven years," Robin recalls. "I was mourning for children so deeply, I had to turn it over to God."

He did not leave them comfortless. Instead He gave them a Scripture: "Thou hast turned for me my mourning into dancing" (Psalm 30:11). Three months later, they adopted their son, Ryan.

For 12 long years they prayed for a daughter, even though their prospects looked bleak. One Sunday, the Lord gave an elderly woman a Scripture for someone in the congregation. Wondering who the words were meant for, the woman stepped to the podium and read, "Thou hast turned for me my mourning into dancing." Vic and Robin knew God was moving on their behalf.

The following week, I met a woman carrying a baby across a grocery store parking lot. She told me that in two days, the little girl would be turned over to the state and undoubtedly sentenced to years of foster care.

I called Vic and Robin and told them about my chance meeting. Ten days later, they drove hundreds of miles to stand before a judge, who granted them custody of the child.

"We hadn't seen our daughter when we went to court," Robin remembers, "but the judge stared at me, bewildered. Then he said, 'I think you're in for a surprise.'

"When they put the baby in my arms, I couldn't believe what I saw! She had my unusual coloring and my own red hair. Between her eyebrows was a birthmark that matched Vic's. I knew it was God's signature. When I looked up, everyone in the courtroom was crying, but I was laughing. My joy was more than complete. God found my baby in a parking lot! He can do anything."

The adoption was finalized several months later. Only the Father of the fatherless could have orchestrated this homecoming. He truly does turn mourning into dancing.

Adoption Resources

• **The Adoption Directory** is a comprehensive guide to state statutes on adoption. Check your local library or write:

Gale Research Inc.
P.O. Box 441914
Detroit, MI 48244-9980
or call toll-free at (800) 877-GALE. Cost of the directory is $55.

• **The National Adoption Center**
1218 Chestnut St.
Philadelphia, PA 19107
(215) 925-0200
Outside Pennsylvania call toll-free (800) TO-ADOPT

A telecommunication network connects agencies around the

country, allowing prospective families and special-needs children to be registered and matched.

• The National Resource Center for Special-Needs Adoption
P.O. Box 337
Chelsea, MI 48118
(313) 475-8693

This center can make a resource referral for special-needs children in your state.

• Adoptive Families of America
3333 Highway 100 N.
Minneapolis, MN 55422
(612) 535-4829

This national adoptive-parent organization, which publishes a bi-monthly magazine, *Ours*, has a 32-page packet of free information for prospective parents.

• The National Committee for Adoption
1930 Seventeenth St. NW
Washington, DC 20009
(202) 328-1200

The committee publishes the *Adoption Factbook*, a summary of state adoption regulations, adoption statistics, current adoption issues, financial considerations, and adoption resources. Cost is $41.95.

• Bethany Christian Services
901 Eastern Ave. N.W.
Grand Rapids, MI 49503
(616) 459-6273

Bethany Christian Services is the nation's leading private adoption agency.

• The American Academy of Adoption Attorneys
P.O. Box 33053
Washington, DC 20033

This national organization has members in 38 states.

• **Academy of California Adoption Lawyers**
926 Garden St.
Santa Barbara, CA 93101
(805) 962-0988

• **Holt International Children's Services**
P.O. Box 2880
Eugene, OR 97402
(503) 687-2202
    This nonprofit organization strives to unite homeless children
from foreign countries with adoptive families in the U.S.

How Much Will an Adoption Cost?

    It can cost thousands of dollars to adopt a child. The least expen-
sive adoptions are through public agencies—usually around $1,000.
Charges for both private agencies and independent placement range
from $5,000 to $15,000. Those fees cover pregnancy and adoption
counseling, medical care, and legal bills. Many private agencies charge
less, relying on contributions to make up the difference. Either way,
make sure the agency or attorney is able to account for the services
rendered.

As a young girl, Melanie Hemry dreamed of raising a family of 13. Instead, she and her husband, Ken, have helped find homes for a dozen children. The Hemrys, who live in Edmond,
Oklahoma, have two adopted daughters: Heather and Lauren.

26

Learning to Live with Pain

Nancy Trout

*I*t was the first day of Christmas vacation for our kids, and I was taking our youngest daughter, Meredith, then nine, to her gymnastics lesson. My husband, Mike, who is co-host of the "Focus on the Family" radio broadcast, would pick her up later while I attended a women's group meeting at our church. I swung our new Mazda 626—Mike's dream car—onto the main boulevard near our Southern California home. We passed one stoplight and continued through the next, but that's where my memory ends.

We later learned that a 16-year-old driver thought she could beat our car through the intersection as she made a left-hand turn across our path. She plowed right into our Mazda—practically a head-on collision. She would be treated for a forehead cut and released. But I knew none of that then. When I came to, I was slumped against the steering wheel, with Meredith's cries bringing me back to reality.

I tried to clear the fog from my brain as searing pain vibrated from my right ankle. I could see a crowd of people peering into the car. I was angry for their intrusion since they merely stood by, staring, but I was more concerned with Meredith. She was crying and afraid, saying her stomach hurt. Just a few minutes before, she had pulled the shoulder harness to one side, since the strap cut into her neck, so her abdominal area had taken the full brunt of the seat belt when she was thrown forward. (Later the police would tell my husband that neither of us would have survived if we hadn't been wearing seat belts.)

When firemen and paramedics arrived, they were able to free Meredith and put her into the ambulance, but they needed 30 minutes for the "Jaws of Life" to open my door. As I waited, listening to the sound of tearing metal and trying to ignore the pain in my ankle, I kept praying for Meredith. At last my door was open, and a paramedic leaned over me.

"Where do you hurt?" he asked.

"My right leg," I answered. From the pain, I knew it had to be broken badly.

"Anything else?"

"Well, my neck hurts a little, too," I replied weakly. That information concerned him more, so the paramedics strapped me to a body board and tied my head down before they gingerly removed me from the car. As soon as I was placed in the ambulance, I lost consciousness.

An Unfamiliar Journey

I awoke in the emergency room. I kept asking the nurses, "Has anyone called my husband?" and they kept nodding yes. Finally, one of them said she would double-check, and sure enough, Mike hadn't been called. They reached him just as he was about to leave to pick up Meredith after gymnastics.

The nurse told him we had been in an accident, but we were all right. Mike rushed to the hospital, mentally replaying the phone conversation. *Did the nurse say they were both all right? Or was just Meredith okay?*

Actually, the doctors were—at the outset—more worried about her possible internal injuries from the seat belt. But when they determined she wasn't in danger, they turned back to me. The X-ray showed no major damage to my neck—just a bad case of whiplash.

The major concern was my right leg, which had been crushed by the impact from the other car. We all knew it was a mess; any first-year medical student could see that. The purple skin with its abrasions was so swollen that all doctors could do was splint the ankle and wait for the swelling to go down before they could operate on it. That would take a full week. The wait gave me plenty of time to think, and I was concerned about more than just my ankle. How would I keep being a good mother to our three daughters? Or a good wife to Mike? Little did I know those worries were well-founded.

The surgery took place on Christmas Eve morning, and for eight hours orthopedic surgeons attempted to put my right ankle back together. The heel bone was crushed, and the ankle was broken in several places. The surgeons removed a bone out of my hip and grafted it into my ankle, then inserted several permanent screws to knit the bones together. Then they took grafts from my right thigh to cover the areas where the foot skin had been rubbed off.

I spent two weeks flat on my back with my ankle encased in a special foam cast that would allow the skin grafts to "take." When I finally was released to go home, I was still weak. I could barely do *anything* myself. Just walking from the bed to the bathroom on crutches was a chore. Mike did as much as he could, but I needed full-time care. That's when our oldest daughter, Rebekah, after her first term of college, insisted on staying with me before she got married. She said it would help her to be home, but I'll never forget what she did for me, spending months at my bedside and keeping the house in order.

I was also amazed how friends from church and Focus on the Family brought meals over every night for several months. What a wonderful help that was.

Walking a New Path

The mundane things in life that I'd always taken for granted—such as taking a bath—suddenly weren't so easy. Just getting me past the glass shower doors and into the tub was an adventure. You should have seen my first bath. Meredith placed a child-sized lawn chair in the front of the tub. Then Mike lifted me past the shower door while I kept my right foot in the air.

Although I was grateful to soak myself in warm water, I let a feeling of helplessness envelop me. I felt useless—I couldn't even get myself into a tub. I looked at my ankle. The swollen, discolored skin was grotesque. I was no longer whole.

I tried to tell myself that my injury was just a broken ankle and that after a season of healing, I could return to a normal life. But as the weeks passed and turned into months, my ankle failed to respond beyond a certain point. Then I had a new concern: Some days I was so discouraged I couldn't even pray. During those times, three close friends prayed for me. Gradually, I came to grips with the idea that I would never again run down a sandy beach or attack a powdery ski slope.

My injuries, of course, pale in significance relative to those of people paralyzed or severely injured in accidents. Not for one moment would I want to compare what I went through to the experiences of those brave people. But one of the few things I share with those folks is the emotional and physical strain of learning to live with pain. My pain may not be as intense as what others experience, but it's certainly gotten my attention. And, unfortunately, it's affected my relationships with Mike, the girls, and close friends because I'm not as patient as I once was. That bothers me.

We've also had to adjust to the idea that I'm not going to be as physically active as I once was. For instance, when I get up in the morning, I limp severely for the first hour or two. It's frustrating to wake up—especially after a poor night's sleep—and know the first thing I'm going to have to deal with is my right ankle. I know it may sound silly to people, but I used to love going barefoot. Now I have to slip some shoes on and get that ankle loosened up before I can walk.

Skiing—whether it's in the mountains or on the lakes—is out of the picture. A couple of years ago, after Focus on the Family moved to Colorado Springs, my family went to one of the state's ski resorts. It wasn't a whole lot of fun being left behind while everyone went skiing. It would have been easier to stay home, but that doesn't promote family togetherness, does it?

I doubt I'll ever be able to play tennis again—not that Steffi Graf ever had anything to worry about. I can walk, but if I stroll for even a couple of miles, I pay for it the rest of the day. And hiking this summer in the Rockies with Mike and the family is impossible because I'm no longer sure-footed. I lose my balance easily, since my ankle has limited movement. What's most frustrating is not being able to carry our young grandson, Christian, up and down stairs when he puts out his little arms to me. I'm always afraid I'll trip and fall.

An Uncertain Future

I say these things not to complain but to illustrate how my life has changed following my accident. What helps the most is concentrating on the good that has come out of it. Mike and I are a lot more aware of the preciousness of life and how quickly it can be gone. When I was wedged in my car in the middle of the intersection, I realized how temporary life on earth really is.

But pain doesn't always allow me to be so thoughtful. Sometimes I think, *This has gone on long enough; let me get on with my life.* That's because I want everything to be taken care of *right now.* I want to do what I used to do; Mike wants me to go places we used to go. We both get frustrated that those things don't happen anymore. The strange thing about a crisis is that it often brings couples closer together at its onset, but as the trauma continues, the constant struggle wears them down. Mike and I have learned that we can't take our relationship for granted but must work at it every day.

My friends often ask me how Mike is taking all of this. When I started my rehabilitation, his first reaction was "put that foot on the floor and walk right." My husband may not be the world's most sympathetic person, but he's also challenged me not to feel sorry for myself.

In 1991, when I started packing our belongings to move to Colorado Springs, I came across a book that had Jeremiah 29:11 on the cover: " 'For I know the plans I have for you,' declares the Lord, 'plans to prosper you and not to harm you, plans to give you hope and a future.' "

Of course, I've heard that verse before, but it really struck me this time. I may never understand why I can't do many of the things I used to do, but the verse tells me that God is here. He loves me, and although He didn't choose to fix my ankle, He will still walk with me every step of the way.

Also, I have a deeper appreciation for my family and my friends. I remember Dr. Dobson saying after his 1990 heart attack that you look at things differently when you've escaped death. *That's so true,* I've thought. Oh, I may not go around thinking, *Boy, today is more precious than yesterday,* but I do realize how quickly life can be taken away.

I think the accident has drawn our family closer. I'll never forget how Rebekah cared for me. Or how Meredith tenderly watches out for me, especially on icy sidewalks. Or how my middle daughter, Amy, was always there when my foot needed rubbing or my spirits needed lifting. Even now when I'm hurting, she takes my arm, and we go for a walk.

Yes, I can still walk, and for that, I am most thankful.

Nancy and Mike Trout live in Colorado Springs.

27

More Than Inner Beauty

Candy Wood

Most girls remember the moment when their mothers at last gave in to their pleas for makeup. I was a seventh-grader when Mom relented—but I had to wear colorless gloss; pink lipstick wasn't allowed until I was a ninth-grade cheerleader. I liked the grown-up way it made me feel . . .

I wear a lot more makeup these days, but my mother doesn't object. That's because my face was taken apart by a surgeon's knife.

In the spring of 1982, I was 30, happily married to Lee, and mother to Elliott, six, and Colley, 23 months. For a year I'd been traipsing to doctor's offices near our home in Birmingham, Alabama. My sinuses constantly drained, and I battled severe headaches. I gulped 12 Tylenol tablets a day for the pain. The year before, I'd even undergone sinus surgery to open up the drainage ducts, but the symptoms persisted.

I visited 14 doctors in all, and each blamed my problems on allergies. But I was having trouble breathing through my right nostril. Finally, I went to another ear-nose-throat specialist who discovered a cyst. He quickly scheduled a biopsy to determine the size and position, as well as a test for malignancy.

The night before the surgery, clinging to Lee's hand, I asked my doctor, "What's the worst thing that can happen to me?"

"You can lose the right side of your face," he sadly replied. "But you asked, 'What's the worst?' Let's hope for the best."

He slipped out of the room. As Lee mumbled "Our lives will never be the same," I went berserk.

Until that moment, I had been stoically accepting the biopsy. Now it pointed to massive surgery and the possibility of *dying*—not being with my husband and not raising our young children. Through my sobs, I insisted on calling other doctors, my parents, the ministers from our church—I wanted everyone to *fix* this right now. The nurses finally gave me a sleeping pill. Lee stayed by my side all night.

In the next morning's biopsy, the doctor made a dramatic discovery: The cyst was actually a large mass perched behind my right eye. Was it malignant? The results were so inconclusive that he sent the tissue to the Mayo Clinic pathology department in Rochester, Minnesota.

The rest of the day was chaotic. Lee and I wanted answers, but the doctors could only speculate on the outcome. Only another sleeping pill stopped my swirling thoughts that night. *How did so many doctors miss it? Why do I have to go through this? What's going to happen to my family?* By the end of the next day, I was wrung out. The realization that I had no control over anything in my life settled around me like a dark cloak.

Finally, in the middle of the night, I said, "All right, Lord. It looks as though I'm going to have to go through this, and I can't go through it without You. You'll just have to take control of my life. It's totally Yours." The circumstances were still the same, but suddenly I felt different. I knew that no matter what lay ahead, He was in control.

Still, not knowing if the tumor was malignant unnerved me. My friends dropped by, and each one tried to be cheerful, but we were all thinking the same thing: cancer.

People find this difficult to believe, but my main worry wasn't over losing my *looks* but my very life. I'd always taken any "cuteness" for granted and was too busy enjoying life and my family to dwell on my face.

One of my doctor friends tried to encourage me about the Mayo Clinic team. "Candy," he said, "they've got this new doctor up there, Dr. Ian Jackson from Scotland. His specialty is deformed children, so if you have to have your face taken apart, at least he can put it back together."

I knew he was trying to console me, but I didn't want to think about the life-and-death risk that would pose. Then word arrived from Mayo. The tumor was malignant. I would, indeed, have to have facial surgery. When I talked with Mayo's Dr. Jackson, he described how he'd cut across the top of my head from ear to ear and then down the front of my face to get to the tumor. Then he added quietly, "You must know that we won't be able to replace the bones to your face. You'll wake up severely deformed and will have only your mouth and left eye intact." If the cancer didn't reoccur, they hoped to start reconstruction in a year.

I impatiently waved all that aside. "I just want to know if I'm going to live through the surgery."

"We'll do all we can to get you through it," he replied.

(I've since talked with other surgeons who assure me that my response was normal. *Life* is the first concern for most head and neck cancer patients.)

I was fairly calm until that night. Then I flipped out. *Tomorrow they're going to take my head apart*, I thought as my emotions ranged all the way from "I'm going to be okay" to "I'm going to die." I dictated detailed funeral arrangements to Lee and my parents and tape-recorded messages to Elliott and Colley so they could remember my voice. And I refused to go to sleep, insisting that if I was going to die the next day, I didn't want to sleep away the few hours I had left.

Somewhere in the middle of the night, though, the Lord's calming presence settled around me again. The next afternoon, moments before the doctors put me under the anesthesia, I told God, "You know what I want, but I'm ready to accept whatever You do."

The operation took nine hours. Later I learned that after Dr. Jackson made the incisions to peel back the right side of my face, he sent each of the removed bones to the lab to be checked for malignancy. Then he carefully cut away the "large mass" that was the size of a baseball.

While he waited for the lab report, he left the operating room to think about the alternatives. Immediate reconstruction had never been accomplished before in this type of cranial surgery. If he didn't try to replace the facial bones, though, only the left side of my face would be intact. The right side would be sunken, and with no bone to hold my right eye in place, I'd lose it.

When the lab report came back that most of the bones were free of malignancy, he decided to try the reconstruction.

When I awakened in the intensive care unit, Lee was holding my hand. "Candy, they got it all." Then he added, "And they put back the bones," but all I wanted to hear was that the cancer was gone. I drifted back to sleep.

My head wasn't bandaged, but Dr. Jackson had prepared Lee for the ear-to-ear stitches and the row that curved around my nose. Since we had been expecting total disfigurement, those were of little consequence. I spent two weeks recuperating and being part of medical students' daily tour, as they examined the miracle of immediate reconstruction.

Still Uphill

Once home, I was still on an emotional, spiritual, and physical roller coaster. One minute I'd be fired up—full of faith, trust, and hope. The next—tired, frightened, and teary.

With Lee, I felt free to complain. With everyone else, I performed. I wanted God to bring His good out of my trauma, and I thought I needed to help Him do that.

Lee, on the other hand, didn't get much rest. Nor did he have anyone to talk to. He wasn't being spiritually built up as I had been. Besides, he was angry. Angry at God, angry at the disruption in our household. He was even angry at me for not being healthy. When we'd talk, I'd ask if he was upset over my scarred face, but he insisted he wasn't. After all, he'd say, at least I had all of it.

Because I had limited energy, my family and friends were always around the house helping with meals, the children, and anything else I needed. While Lee appreciated everyone's kindness, he wanted to come home after work, put on his robe, and relax. I thrived on the company.

After a few weeks, before we could settle into a routine, the facial pain began. Next, I started losing a pound a day. After being home only seven months, I had to go back to Minnesota.

Dr. Jackson quickly realized that several of my facial bones were filled with infection. The next five weeks were even more intense than my first surgery as the medical team fought to clean up the infection while removing as few bones as possible. In those 35 days, I had four more major surgeries. It seemed that every few days they were taking away more of my head and moving me closer to disfigurement. Each time Lee arrived for a weekend visit, I looked different: My forehead was sunken, and patches of scalp were moved from the back of my head to protect the vulnerable forehead area. Skin grafts from my thighs were at the back and side of my head, leaving me with two major bald spots.

But, amazingly, as difficult as those five weeks were, I was the closest I had ever been to the Lord. Perhaps I kept remembering that I still had my face and the sight in my right eye. But I think I was just buoyed by prayers—not only my own, but those of my friends as well.

I didn't look much like a victor though. My weight had dropped to 79 pounds because of my inability to eat well, and my sallow skin hung on my bones. My shaven head was covered with railroad tracks of stitches.

One of the immediate things I tried to do when I returned home after those traumatic five weeks was buy a wig. It really was too soon; my head wasn't healed yet. But Lee and one of our friends took me anyway. It was a terrible experience. None of the wigs looked like me. They were all too poofy or too lacquered or too thick or too something. As much as Lee tried to tell me I looked fine, he couldn't convince me. I felt frustrated, disappointed, and angry. I took the final wig off and threw it at the mirror. "If you want to buy it, fine," I snapped. "But I'm not going to wear it."

Lee was astounded. "You've had massive surgeries and are handling disfigurement. Why is *this* so difficult for you?"

I wasn't sure I could explain it to him, but I tried. "Because I didn't have a choice with any of that. I have a choice here, and I choose *not* to wear one!" And with that, I put my little cloth shower cap back on.

A few evenings later, before a church supper, friends came over with a box of scarves. Big ones, little ones, bright ones, and solid ones.

They wrapped my head in a bright red scarf, then tied a black-and-white one into a side bow. I loved the festive look, especially since it made me appear less pitiful.

Lee hated the scarves. He liked wigs, saying they looked more *normal*. I argued that I hated them. They made me feel dumpy and ugly. Lee said I wore the scarves to get attention. I replied that I wore them because they gave color to my face and were cooler. I continued to wear them; Lee continued to grumble.

Eventually, I became comfortable with wearing a wig. But what helped the most was finding a toupee manufacturer who would make hairpieces not only to cover the skin grafts, but also to blend into my own hair. Now, that was my idea of normal.

A New Crisis

By now I was being asked by numerous churches to give my testimony, which I loved doing. I was still having a hard time dealing with pain and fatigue, as well as the fear of recurrence. But in my talks, I tended not to tell about those times. I described the good things.

One night as I was leaving to speak, Lee bitterly said, "When you're telling them how *blessed* you've been, don't include me!"

I looked at him in amazement. I'd survived massive brain surgery, five weeks of bone infection, and more surgeries. How could he *not* see the blessing? Mad as a hornet, I left the house in tears. That night, I told my usual bright testimony.

Because I was talking about the Lord with anyone who would listen, I soon became everyone's counselor. Night after night, Lee would overhear calls I received from strangers. I felt I couldn't ask them to wait until morning. Resentment was growing in both of us.

One evening, everything exploded. Lee snapped at me as we were discussing plans for the week. "You've got time for everyone but me," he railed. Before I knew it, he was yelling and kicking some boxes I had packed for Goodwill. Clothes scattered with each swing of his leg. He was totally out of control, and I was afraid. He stormed out of the bedroom, his face red with rage.

When he returned, he collapsed in the chair. With his head buried in his hands, he moaned, "I need help."

The next morning, Lee called for information about a support group. Problems were handled in this group more from a psychological viewpoint than a spiritual standpoint, but it was a beginning of healing for him and understanding for me. I learned that he needed my time and attention. He learned he had bottled up his fears and questions and used anger to express his frustration at our lives' disruption. But most of all, the group helped us concentrate on what we had *left*.

Helping the Children

As much as I would have loved to have protected my children, they were definitely affected by my illness. Elliott's teacher was often lenient with him when I was away at the Mayo Clinic. Picking up on what seemed to be favoritism, the other children resented him. By the time Elliott was in the fifth grade, we noticed he was having difficulty fitting in. Quiet and sensitive, he didn't have many friends. Once, after I spoke at an elementary girls' Bible study, I received a letter from one of his classmates. She wrote, "In the first grade we were jealous of the attention Elliott always got from the teacher. Now I see why, and I'm sorry."

Colley continues to be extremely protective of me. When she was in kindergarten, I occasionally ate lunch with her. One afternoon, as we walked out of the lunchroom, I noticed her usually happy little face streaked with tears. "That boy just said you have an ugly nose, Mom."

When I talked to the teacher, she let me explain to the class why I looked the way I did. The children were so intrigued by how I tape my hair on every morning that Colley wanted me to come to "Show and Tell" the next week with my hairpieces.

Let's Face It

I'm often asked how I handle the loss of my "looks." That's a legitimate question, especially from those who know I skipped my college classes one morning when I awakened with two blemishes. But my face represents who I am now. It reminds me of how the Lord spared my life and how I've learned to trust my future to Him. I wouldn't *refuse* the old face if it was offered back, but only if I could have the new heart, too.

As I began to heal, I remembered the women on the plastic surgery floor of the Mayo Clinic. Many accepted the fact they were deformed; often they didn't even bother with basic makeup. I didn't like the pitying looks my visitors gave me, so while I was there, I'd put on blush and a bit of lipstick just so I looked healthier.

When I returned home and was trying to accent any positive features I had left—to detract from my scarred and lopsided face—I remembered my college theater days. There we had used makeup techniques to change our age. Why couldn't I use the same techniques to make myself feel better? Soon I was eager to share what I'd learned with other women.

Every time I returned to the Mayo Clinic, I tried to encourage other women not to give in to their disfigurement, but to find ways—whether through wigs, hats, scarves, or makeup—to draw attention away from their injuries. I decided that the best way to help would be to make a video for hospitals to use on their facial surgery floors. I asked two friends I'd met at Mayo Clinic, Bonnie Shelley and Martha Bemner, to help. Bonnie's face was crushed in an auto accident, and Martha's skin was absolutely fried in a plane crash. Both were excited to help other patients.

When we filmed the video "Let's Face It," we didn't use the words "beautiful" or "pretty." Instead, we said "healthy." Our dressing and makeup suggestions aren't for vanity; they're for self-esteem. How a woman looks is one of the few things left in her control during treatment. One thing I always stress is that while the techniques may help, they don't *change* our conditions. My faith in the Lord is the source of my own strength and hope, but I found that before I could get healthier, I had to *feel* healthier.

Today I'm free of the cancer, but I remain in constant pain from the scar tissue. Despite everything that has happened, I've learned not to dwell on the bad days. I'm convinced that God allows certain things to happen in our lives, and if we allow Him to, He can, as it says in Romans 8:38, "make all things work together for good for those who love the Lord and who are called according to his purpose."

When we put our confidence in looks, that can be taken away. My confidence has long been in Jesus Christ, but I'm more confident than ever because I know He can't be taken away.

Know Someone Who Needs Help?

Two videos are available: "Let's Face It: Makeup" and "Let's Face It: Hair Loss." Each costs $27, which includes shipping and handling. Write: Illustrated Care, Inc., 5300 Cahaba River Rd., Suite 250, Birmingham, Alabama 35243.

The Woods live in Birmingham, Alabama.

28

When Couples Say "I Don't"

Bob Welch

he bailiff announces, "All rise." The gavel falls, the judge sits down, the trial begins. Six years ago in a church, the couple had said "I do" to each other. Now, in the stark coldness of a courtroom, they begin the painful process of saying "I don't."

Sitting within 15 feet of each other, the man and woman avoid eye contact. Though legally still married, they have become petitioner and respondent, not husband and wife; enemies, not allies. The connection between them is as lifeless as the bricks in the courtroom walls.

And to think that they once called each other sweetheart.

We've all watched a marriage begin, but few of us have watched a marriage end. From the back row, I've come to witness one of the thousands of divorce wars fought every weekday in courtrooms across America. It isn't pretty. But to understand the importance of wearing a seat belt, sometimes you need to see the mangled car.

This couple is your typical middle-class family. They're nice-looking, and they dress well. They aren't dealing with emotional turmoil

213

from having grown up in alcoholic or abusive families. They're simply a couple who decided to split because of "irreconcilable differences."

A judge will decide who gets what, from their house to the *Funk & Wagnalls* encyclopedias. But the *big* question is: Who will receive custody of their three-year-old son?

As the trial unfolds, a chasm of contrasts separates then and now, wedding and dissolution. The two are flanked not by a best man and maid of honor bearing rings that will unite, but by attorneys armed with evidence that will divide.

There is no photographer capturing each priceless memory, only a court reporter recording each verbal volley.

There is no triumphant music, only the tiny sound of testimony spoken into microphones.

There is no festive throng of family and friends, only empty benches and a handful of supporters waiting in the lobby.

Between sessions, the two gather with their friends and families in the lobby, like boxers going to their respective corners for advice and encouragement.

The woman's attorney argues that the man is an irresponsible parent, as shown by the raising of his 12- and 14-year-old sons (children from a previous marriage) who lived with the couple. He doesn't believe in structure and discipline. He doesn't care if the kids do their homework. The woman, the attorney says, has cared enough to set boundaries, build structure, and require accountability.

The man's attorney counterattacks. He argues that the woman has been abusive to the children. She has hit them, screamed at them, locked them out of the house in their underwear. The man, he says, has cared enough to help the boys with their homework, calmly handle friction, and cook an abundance of meals, particularly pancake breakfasts.

The topics range from who dented the car to who was responsible for the older boy stapling the cat. These are the subjects that will decide which parent will be best for a little boy who has no say in the matter.

At one point, the woman is on the witness stand. "You talk about a time when your husband put you into a bedroom," says her husband's attorney.

"He *threw* me into the bedroom, yes."

"Do you remember why you were placed in the bedroom by him?"

"He was angry at me."

"Do you know why?"

"No."

"Wasn't it because he just separated you from a fight with one of the older children?"

"No."

Minute-by-minute, hour-by-hour, day-by-day, the evidence grows like a gnarly tree. The judge hears about the time the three-year-old, whom we'll call Kenny, was slapped for pushing the VCR buttons during *The Little Mermaid.* The time he cried when being shifted from one parent to another. The time he was allowed to ride in the back of a pickup truck. And another time when he was slapped.

"She came home from work—I was preparing dinner—and she came in the door swearing at me about leaving a porch light on," the man testifies. "Kenny had the refrigerator door open and was standing there with a cup in his hands. She came in, put her coat on the chair, and reached for a V-8 in the refrigerator. She pulled the door away from Kenny, and he said, 'I hate you.' She started yelling, and then she slapped him."

The woman listens, shaking her head. What's true? What's not? Amid this family's chaos, it's difficult to tell. While the battle continues, the propaganda war heats up, each side describing incidents in vastly different ways.

A handful of witnesses say the man is the one who took care of Kenny. He changed the boy, fed him, held him, played with him. Then the woman's brother takes the stand. "She did everything for Kenny," he testifies.

For a few days, the two older boys' friends—ranging from age nine to 14—come to testify. They gather excitedly in the lobby, as if on a Cub Scout field trip. But their moods grow serious when, one by one, they are brought into the courtroom; nervous kids in dress shirts, ties, and Nikes. Innocent kids caught in the cross fire of warring adults.

Timid, their words on the witness stand are barely discernible. While cross-examining the boys, the woman's attorney impatiently taps his fingertips together. He places verbal land mines to trip up witnesses who step in the wrong spot and, for those still unscathed, fires a machine-gun of questions to crack their credibility. Then, one by one, the stepsons are called to the stand.

"You don't like your stepmother, do you?" he asks the man's 14-year-old.

"No, sir."

"You didn't like her because she was the one who had rules in the house while your dad didn't. Isn't that true?"

"No, sir."

"Your dad didn't make you go to bed at any certain time, did he?"

"Yes, sir, he did."

"He didn't make you do your homework, did he?"

"Sir, he did."

"If he made you do homework, why did you get so many incompletes and F's?"

Between sessions, one of the young witnesses looks at the stockpiled ammunition on the attorneys' tables—piles of notes and documents.

"This," says the youngster, "is a mess."

When the seven-day trial finally ends, the court reporter has typed the equivalent of 1,400 double-spaced pages. The judge has listened to 30 witnesses. The attorneys have entered 110 pieces of evidence, everything from belts allegedly used for hitting to father-son photographs. And the man and woman have spent about $35,000 in attorney's fees; one attorney charges $95 an hour, the other $145.

Two weeks after the trial ends, the judge, "with considerable trepidation," grants custody of the child to the mother and gives the father liberal visitation rights. In his decision, he mentions a recent case in which the state had to remove a child from the care of a mildly retarded man and woman. The couple had tried courageously to overcome their handicaps and be good parents, but it was not within their capacity.

"How sad," the judge says, "that two mentally sound people can hardly do better."

Then he adds, "I hope I never see another case like this one."

As the courtroom empties and the parties head for their new, readjusted lives, I think what it must have been like six years ago when the man and woman vowed to love each other in sickness and in health, in good times and bad, till death do they part. I wonder how the same people who made those vows could have become such bitter enemies. I wonder if it was all worth it; if divorce is, indeed, the mender of wounds that it was hailed as in the 1970s. And, finally, I wonder about the collateral damage of ending a marriage in the trenches of a trial.

What has this taught the older children about how adults solve family problems? And what will become of the three-year-old boy who, as the judge says in his decree, has been "ping-ponged" between two feuding parents?

The sad irony is this: The time and place to prove one's proficiency as a parent isn't during a divorce proceeding in front of a judge, but in a family setting in front of the children themselves. For all the time, money, and energy that went into this trial, all it really proved was the high cost of divorce—both in money and in human casualties.

The little boy was right. This *has been* a mess. "Divorce court is worse than war," another witness says when it's all over. "In war, at least you have a winner."

Bob Welch is a features writer for the *Register-Guard* newspaper in Eugene, Oregon, where he lives with his wife, Sally, and two sons, Ryan and Jason. This article is adapted from Bob's first book, *More to Life Than Having It All.* Published by Harvest House.

Divorce: At What Cost?

Researchers are finding that the effects of divorce span several generations, according to a recent article in *American Demographics* magazine.

- On average, children of divorced parents are less educated than others their age, according to Louisiana State University demographer Jiang Hong Li.
- Both white and black children who grow up in broken families are less likely to graduate from high school than children with similar backgrounds who grow up in intact families, adds Hong Li. White children of divorce are also less likely to achieve a high-status occupation.
- Children of divorce leave home earlier than others, but not to form families of their own, say Brown University demographers Roger Avery, Frances Goldschieder, and

Alden Speare, Jr. They are far more likely than their peers to live together before marrying, adds University of Michigan demographer Arland Thornton. And once they do marry, they are more likely to divorce.

- The poverty rate for children living in single-parent homes is five times the rate for children living with two parents.

- Divorced men experience an average 42 percent rise in their standard of living in the first year after divorce, while divorced women (and their children) experience a 73 percent decline.

- Children of divorce are 20 percent to 40 percent more likely to develop health problems than children in intact families. They also are more likely to be injured accidentally—the leading cause of childhood death and disability.

- School-age children living with a parent and stepparent, or divorced mother only, are 40 percent to 75 percent more likely to repeat a grade and 70 percent more likely to be expelled from school.

- Children who grow up in fractured families are less likely to graduate from high school than children from intact families.

- Children of fractured families experience significantly lower self-esteem than children of intact families.

- A disproportionate number of runaway teens come from stepparent households.

- Children of divorce have higher rates of delinquency.

- Young sons often experience nightmares and a "father hunger" soon after the dad leaves home. In their teens, they are more likely to have increased levels of aggression, gang membership, and other emotional and behavioral problems.

- Young daughters of divorce often experience anxiety and guilt. In their teens, they are more likely to be sexually involved, marry younger, be pregnant more often before marriage, and become divorced or separated from their eventual husbands.

- Children of divorce typically experience depression, drug

and alcohol experimentation, and a diminished ability to form lasting relationships.
- Children in single-parent homes usually receive less parental attention, affection, and supervision than children in two-parent families.

From *Free to be Family*, published by the Family Research Council based in Washington, D.C.

When Divorce Happens Later in Life

Joy had the perfect marriage. She married her childhood sweetheart, Bill, when she was 20 and fresh out of Bible school. Handsome and a natural leader, Bill became an ordained minister, specializing in church planning.

For 35 years Joy worked alongside him, raising their four children, teaching Sunday school, organizing church music programs, and playing the piano in services. If anyone had asked, she would have said they had a happy marriage.

Then, a week before Mother's Day, Joy found a letter addressed to her in their mailbox. Without discussion or warning, Bill wrote that he was leaving her. Their children were grown, he said, and his responsibilities at home were over. He wanted a new life without her.

"It was like a death," Joy recalls. "The only trouble is that the funeral is still never over for me."

Stuck financially and devastated emotionally, Joy needed five years to work through the pain and anger she felt over Bill's departure.

"I'd known him since I was 13," she says. "I'd never even kissed anyone else."

Why do seemingly stable men like Bill divorce their wives and devastate their families just when the children have left the nest? Why, when the financial burdens have ebbed and the "golden years" of retirement are just around the corner?

Dr. Archibald Hart, a psychology professor and author of *Healing Adult Children of Divorce*, calls the culprit "later-life crisis."

Most divorces occur within eight or 10 years of marriage, Hart says, but increasingly, later-in-life divorces happen after a couple have been married 25 or 30 years.

"The empty nest occurs later now because people are marrying later and delaying having children," explains Hart. "For some couples, the sixties are becoming the newly recaptured years. But the home environment begins to get stale." Husbands and wives who have devoted themselves to their children, their jobs, and even church work—to the exclusion of keeping their personal relationship alive— may find they hardly know each other once their outside responsibilities decline. When the couple doesn't have a compelling reason to stay together, says Dr. Hart, one spouse or the other may begin to look outside the marriage for a relationship.

Hart lists these warning signs for older couples who may be vulnerable:

- The man is bored with his job and feels unfulfilled
- The children have scattered, isolating the parents
- They have no special "togetherness" as a couple
- The marriage has a long history of conflict

Hart says that prevention for late divorce should occur throughout a marriage, as couples keep the spark of romance alive over the years.

"Couples who have fun together and have similar interests and activities hardly ever split up. But when she does her thing and he does his, there can be trouble later on," he says.

For older couples who suddenly find they don't have much in common, Hart suggests thinking back on the courtship and early marriage years and trying to rebuild the togetherness that existed then.

So far, the later-life crisis seems to be a male phenomenon. Hart says that while older women can embark on long-held goals such as going back to school or starting careers, men in their sixties, on the other hand, start to feel indifferent about their jobs and complacent about their marriages. They aren't ready to retire, but they're tired of working. That's when they panic about aging and develop a "last-chance" mentality to recapture their youth.

Highly successful men are especially vulnerable, Hart says, because they spend a lot of time away from their spouses, plus they often associate with younger women in the business world. "The opportunity for an affair presents itself even to men who aren't looking for it," Hart says. "The higher up the totem pole you are—and this could be a senior pastor or a corporate vice president—the more arrogance and lack of accountability you've tended to develop."

When long-married couples split up, their grown children must deal with the loss of their ideals about a stable family. They often experience role reversal, especially when their mother is left behind in a financial bind and they must care for her. Often an adult child's father image is shattered, too.

"For many people, the father is their God image, their idol," Hart says. "They find they have to detach themselves from their father, and they begin to lose respect for him."

Joy's grown children still struggle with their father's decision. "We were the perfect family at church. When that fell apart, it really hurt them," she says.

Last year, Joy married a widower at a celebration that included all her children and grandchildren. She says the anger over Bill's departure has faded with time. Still, she struggles at family gatherings. "It's just the feeling that there's a dream out there about what my life was supposed to be like," she says. "That dream was shattered."

—Karen E. Klein

❧29

How to Enjoy Your Elderly Parents

Barbara Crosley

Like much of the nation, I was shocked to read a couple of years ago about the Saturday night at an Idaho racetrack when a custodian, making his rounds to lock up, came upon an old man sitting placidly in a wheelchair. He was wearing a brand-new sweatsuit, blue bedroom slippers, and a baseball cap inscribed with "Proud to Be an American." A typewritten note identified him as "John King," a retired farmer suffering from Alzheimer's disease.

In reality, the man was John Kingery, 82, a former autoworker from Portland, Oregon. His daughter had apparently removed him from a Portland nursing home and driven him 300 miles east, where she dumped him.

How terrible to be abandoned by one's own flesh and blood! What would drive a grown child to commit such treachery? A long-held grudge? Greed over the estate? Exhaustion from contending with the parent's ever-worsening disease? Caregiver burnout?

"Granny-dumping" is on the rise, say observers such as Dr. Robert Anzinger, past president of the American College of Emergency Physicians, who estimates that between 100,000 and 200,000 elderly people are left on the doorsteps of hospitals every year. Whoever brought them there quickly speeds away, leaving nurses and other staff to figure out identity, insurance coverage, and a plan for the future.

And while we may shake our heads in dismay, we must also admit that our own parents have not always received unlimited patience, love, and attention from us. While most of us would never commit a desperate act (we think), we have occasionally given in to exasperation. We've cut phone calls short, forgotten to write, or scolded for actions we thought unwise . . . and then felt guilty, remembering how much *they* put up with when *we* were little and dependent.

Deep in our hearts, we want these to be the golden years, times full of laughter and love and sentiment. We want to be able to look back with no regrets. To do so, of course, requires some specific actions now.

If you're going to be visiting your parents or in-laws this holiday season—especially those past the "active senior" stage—here are a few suggestions:

Shift into a Lower Gear

For those of us who've been addicted to the adrenal high of car pools, music lessons, holiday baking, gift shopping, and daily errands (plus work outside the home), the slower pace of elderly parents can be difficult to adopt. My mother, now 83 but still living alone, can be an exercise in patience when I'm helping her get dressed to leave the house. I've learned to take my time and remember that doing even the most mundane tasks takes longer.

Remember Gift No. 1: Our Time

The elderly, if they are still mentally alert, intuitively know that the sands of time are about to reach the other end of the hourglass. Just before my dad died, when he was confined to home, I remember sitting with him at the kitchen table while we carved a melon for

Sunday dinner. We filled it with cut-up fruit and then arranged a beautiful tray of cold cuts. We laughed, we visited, we teased each other, and we told jokes. I can't remember any great thing we did that afternoon, but I remember that time at the kitchen table like it was yesterday.

Keep Touching

When I'm standing and Mother is sitting, I often place my hand on her shoulder. Physical touching says, "I care." Can you trim toenails? Offer an arm while on a stroll? Rub your mom's feet and legs with lotion? Hold your dad's elbow while you open the car door? At night, I tuck Mother into bed and plant a kiss on her forehead before I go to the guest room. Whenever I can, I touch that precious person!

Shop for Your Parents

Have you ever looked into the refrigerators of the elderly? They're often bare. I take canned foods and fresh perishables on my visits to Mother. I also do most of her clothes shopping as well. I'll often gift-wrap each item so she has the joy of unwrapping each "present."

Plan a Family Reunion

This will often give your elderly mother or father something to look forward to. If possible, ask them to help in the planning. Perhaps they can address envelopes or help organize the activities. Our family reserves the church fellowship hall for our reunions, where we have plenty of room to eat, play table games, and visit.

Ask About the Past

Often, an elderly parent can better remember a cross-country move 50 years ago than what he or she had for breakfast that morning. My father *loved* talking about his childhood, and I can still recall the evening he listed all the cars he ever owned, from the 1916 Overland Chummy Roadster to the '84 Ford pickup he drove just before he died.

Take Trips Together

I once took Dad to Boothill Museum in Dodge City, Kansas, where walking past all the pre-1940 washing machines unleashed a flood of memories for him. He pointed to one of the old wooden ones and proudly said his folks used one just like it. When he walked past an old churn, he asked our children if they knew what it was. They didn't.

My husband and I called Mother a few years ago and said we wanted to drive her back to where she grew up: the tiny town of Newkirk, Oklahoma. When we walked up to the old, one-room schoolhouse, she insisted we take a picture of her standing in the front door. We also visited numerous relatives, many of whom she hadn't seen in decades. She still talks about that trip.

Capture Early Memories

This Christmas, I plan to finish writing my life story. I've been calling Mother, asking for details of various events, like the time I went to the barn to feed the milk cows. As I lowered the half-bushel bucket from the hook, I discovered a snake coiled inside! Mother said she heard a scream and a bucket hit the floor. When I ran to her, she wrapped her arms around me—and told me *she* had put the dead snake there! Such anecdotes are too good to let pass into forgetfulness.

Understand That You May Have to Carry the Load

Much of the visiting and caring for an elderly parent may fall on you, especially if you are a daughter. That's not necessarily the way it *should* be—and there certainly are families with devoted and attentive sons—but don't let your attitude sour into, "Why isn't so-and-so helping out?" Just give the gift of love to the one who gave you so much in years gone by.

If You Can't Visit, Write or Call Regularly

When my mother was hospitalized last May, I felt badly about having to stay with my job 300 miles away. What could I do to let her know I still cared?

I decided to send a card or write a short letter every day for two and a half weeks—18 notes in all. I didn't view it as a large effort on my part, but in phone conversations with Mother later on, she reminded me time after time how much those letters lifted her spirits.

There's almost no excuse for not keeping in steady phone contact these days. Many of the long-distance phone services charge around 10 to 15 cents a minute for evening and weekend phone calls—a real bargain. Whether near or far, a call will lift an elderly parent's spirits.

Recently, I phoned Mother early one Saturday. She hadn't been able to get going that morning, which depressed her. After a warm chat, she felt much better. Then just before we said good-bye, she said, "Barbara, your call made my day!"

Her comment stayed in my heart the rest of *my* day.

Barbara Crosley is permissions editor of *Focus on the Family* magazine.

30

Keepsakes of Sorrow and Comfort

Becky Smith-Greer

When Becky Smith-Greer was growing up in North Carolina, she pretended she was Princess Rose and would someday marry the man of her dreams. Following a college romance, she married Sonny Smith, who became more than the husband of her fairy-tale fantasy. Sonny became her best friend and the loving father of their two children.

The Smiths became teachers in the Hendersonville, North Carolina, area. Sonny was the high school band director, and Becky taught kindergarten.

Then Becky's idyllic life was shattered when she heard the words: "There's been an accident!"

In one swift moment, she lost half her family—her husband and 12-year-old son, Greg—in a plane crash. Two others also perished: Sonny's 26-year-old nephew, Richard, and his bother-in-law, Jack, the pilot of the single-engine craft.

229

Grief was like quicksand, sucking Becky into its inescapable pit. Fear, denial, and panic were followed by numbness and shock. Then came the unbearable pain.

Becky's love for Tonya, her 8-year-old daughter, drove her to search for healing and recovery. Our story begins five months later.

Like a mother tenderly covering her sick child with a soft blanket, spring came gently to the mountains. As the days grew warmer, I realized it was time to begin thinking about the money contributed by the community to a memorial fund for Sonny and Greg. I discussed the matter with the band seniors and Sue Buttner, a good friend. We decided to establish the Marion O. Smith Memorial Music Award at East High and the Marion Gregory Smith Memorial Art Award at Flat Rock Junior High.

The music award was to be a trophy given to a senior band member. His or her peers would vote for the one person who most exemplified the qualities Sonny felt important in a band member: dependability, enthusiasm, loyalty, and a willingness to work.

Greg's award would be a trophy, too; it would be given to the most promising art student selected by the art teacher at Flat Rock Junior High. Sonny's oldest brother, Paul, owned a trophy business, so we commissioned him to design the trophies.

That settled, I concentrated on my own classroom. As the days grew warmer, yellow daffodils blossomed, and spring fever attacked the schoolchildren. Their noise level and energy rose like sap in the trees. Their concentration soared out the window like birds in flight.

One warm day in May, diminutive Sam Jones and I were sitting at a worktable in back of the classroom. Sam was struggling to distinguish the differences in objects pictured on a work sheet, an important prereading skill he usually enjoyed. This day, however, the distractions were too many for him.

A bluebird on the porch railing chirped through the open door. A slight breeze ruffled the window curtains. Some children were playing in the housekeeping center; others were building a city with the wooden blocks. Catherine and Beth were measuring water at the water table. Sam wanted to be anywhere but with me. He fidgeted and poked the air with his pencil.

"What do you see, Sam?" I asked impatiently.

Sensing my frustration, he leaned back in his chair and flashed a big, I-dare-you-not-to-love-me grin.

"Come on, Sam. You've got to finish this before you can go to recess," I pleaded, avoiding his big, blue eyes.

Obediently, Sam leaned down and pored over the work sheet of insects, straining to find the one that was different.

"Look here, Sam. Look here," I finally said, jabbing my finger up and down on the correct one.

Little Sam looked down again, then up at me. His big eyes sparkled mischievously as he broke into a huge, clownlike smile, revealing two missing front teeth.

"Well," he said slowly in pure mountain brogue, "he's a cute little ol' booger, ain't he?"

I burst out laughing. Sam laughed, too. For the first time since the accident, I laughed. Deep, belly-wrenching laughter. I laughed and laughed hysterically.

Ann, my co-teacher, came running. "Becky, what's going on?"

Suddenly the laughter turned to tears. I started to sob as Ann quickly ushered the children outside. Laying my head down, I wept uncontrollably as all the emotions I had been stuffing inside for months came pouring out. I cried until I could cry no more. Grief was like quicksand, always shifting.

The Missing Pieces

As the spring days drifted by, a compelling need surfaced inside me. I became obsessed with knowing why the airplane had crashed. Mike Corbet, a friend from college days, secured a copy of the Federal Aviation Administration's investigative report for me. Somehow I needed to fill in the missing pieces.

After lunch on Mother's Day, Tonya and I drove to Winkler Aviation, a small, private airport near our Hendersonville home. I hoped someone might be able to explain the dynamics of how a plane flies or what causes one to crash.

The airport held a lot of memories for me. Sonny, Greg, Tonya, and I had sometimes taken short pleasure trips around the city when special promotions were offered. Sonny loved flying and was always fascinated with airplanes.

After we parked the car, we went straight to the airport office, hurrying past the small airplanes resting on the runway. A black-haired man in blue coveralls walked out to meet us.

"Can I help you, ma'am?" he asked pleasantly.

"I'd like to see Mr. Winkler, if I may," I replied.

"He's not here right now. I'd be glad to help if I can."

"No," I mumbled, trying to hide my disappointment, "I just wanted to ask him some questions."

As I turned to leave, the man startled me by asking, "You're Mrs. Smith, aren't you?"

"Well, yes," I replied.

"Mrs. Smith," he said, "I'm Mr. Duncan. I've worked at this airport for years. I know about the accident that killed your husband and son. I might be able to answer your questions."

"Oh, Mr. Duncan, I was never able to look at the airplane. Now I need to know what happened."

"Mrs. Smith, my daughter was one of Mr. Smith's students. She loved him. After the accident, I wanted to know what happened, so I flew to Florida and examined the wreckage. I think I can tell you what you want to know.

"The way I understand it," he explained, "they were flying low to take pictures over Sonny's parents' house. As they tried to gain altitude, they got caught in a downdraft and couldn't generate enough speed or power to pull out of it. The engines stalled, and the plane nose-dived into the ground. It was like hitting a brick wall at 180 miles per hour."

"Mr. Duncan, did Greg know what was happening?" I asked.

"No, ma'am, I don't believe so. It was all over in about five seconds."

"Did they suffer?"

"I don't think they could have. The impact was so great; they all died instantly. Their bodies couldn't take the trauma."

My emotions were screaming, *No, I don't want to hear this.* But my mind was saying, *They didn't suffer. My little Greg didn't suffer. He did not lie in the wreckage half conscious and racked with pain. He took one breath here and the next one in eternity.* I wept openly as I listened.

"Mr. Duncan, thank you for your time. You've helped me tremendously," I said, shaking his hand.

"We loved Mr. Smith," he said. "We appreciated what he meant to our daughter and what he did for our school and community, Mrs. Smith. We grieve, too."

In the days following our conversation, I found myself repeatedly saying, "Thank You, God, that they didn't suffer. Thank You; thank You."

Turning a Corner

As the fall days drifted by, I felt myself getting weaker. My emotions were like a stormy ocean; they were becoming more turbulent by the hour as incessant waves of grief were pounding the life out of me. My will to survive was almost gone.

When I lay down at night, the fear of someone breaking in to harm Tonya and me was ever present. I was still haunted by Sonny's empty place beside me. When I tried to sleep, visions of blood and twisted metal often invaded my dreams.

One night I woke up screaming as I saw the plane hurtling downward in my dreams. I could see Greg's eyes filled with terror when he cried out and grabbed for his daddy. For a moment, I was unable to move; my heart pounded violently. Perspiration bathed my body, and I could barely breathe.

Finally I threw back the covers and stumbled through the darkness to Greg's room. A tiny light streamed from his clock radio, casting shadows across his empty bed. I crumbled to the floor beside it and cried into the pillow. In utter desperation, I screamed aloud, "God, if You're there, and if You're real, You've got to help me! I can't go on like this!"

Total darkness enveloped my soul as thoughts of suicide began crawling around inside my mind. I waited for God to show Himself to me. The silence, however, was broken only by the sound of my own sobs as the night disappeared into morning.

Not long after that frightful night, God did come to visit me in an unexpected time and place. He slipped quietly down beside me on the steps of my classroom and used a little boy named Mark to teach me about Himself.

Halloween drew near. The children's nervous energy was fueled by their excitement over Halloween. They jumped around like a herd of kangaroos.

To release some of their pent-up energy, Ann and I took them out for afternoon recess. Some children ran to the swings, others to the see-saws. Several boys raced for the towering oak tree to check on the warrior ants.

Suddenly shrill screams pierced the air. "Go away, Mark! Mrs. Smith, make Mark leave us alone. He's bothering us." I looked up to see Mark chasing several girls with a stick.

Mark was so tiny, I didn't think he had the strength to hurt them. Actually, I was glad to see him interacting at any level. Mark was my puzzle and challenge. His frail body was spaghetti thin, his brown eyes hauntingly blank. In the classroom, he usually sat on the floor, folded his bony knees together, and stared at the carpet. The only way I could look into his eyes was to pull him to me and cup his face in my hands. Even then, he would not look directly at me.

The school nurse had told me that his parents were mentally handicapped and had almost let him starve to death when he was a baby. His mother would simply forget to feed him. Another nurse marked his bottles with a magic marker and taught the mother to feed him by certain television programs. His little body still showed the effects of the neglect.

Mark became my special project. I was determined to discover the person hiding behind the mask of fright. I lavished him with love and attention and watched eagerly for any sign of progress.

"Mark, honey, the girls don't like you chasing them," I tried to explain, stooping down to put my arms around him. "Why don't you go help the boys under the tree? They're watching the ant army."

"Okay," he said and ran off to join them.

A few moments later, I heard it again, "Mrs. Smith, Mark's messing up our ants."

"Mark, come here," I said.

This time he looked squarely at me and ran the other way, straight into the middle of a kickball game.

"Mark!" I said sternly, scooping him up in my arms when I finally caught him.

"Put me down!" he screamed, kicking his feet and flailing his arms. "Put me down!"

"Mark, stop it."

"Put me down," he howled. He continued to create such a scene that I took him away from the playground. He kicked and screamed as I carried him back to our building. The more he carried on, the tighter I held him.

"Mark, I am not going to turn you loose until you quit acting this way. Just calm down," I said softly.

I sat down on the steps of the building and clutched him tightly to my breast. "Mark, honey, you know you're so special to me. I love you. I think you're such a fine little fellow, and I don't like to see you acting this way." I felt him relax a bit.

"You know, Mark, I had a little boy just like you. His name was Greg, but I don't have him anymore. He died." Mark looked up at me now as I talked. "Greg loved Matchbox cars. Do you like those cars?"

He nodded his head vigorously.

"I'll tell you what I'm going to do. Tomorrow I'll bring you one of Greg's cars. Would you like that? I know Greg would like you to have one."

Mark nodded again and gently relaxed. I felt some of the fight drain out of him. I began to hum and rock. In a while, his body went limp as he fell asleep. I cradled him in my arms and wiped the perspiration from his tiny forehead.

Ever so quietly, God crept into my heart and whispered softly, "Becky, you're just like Mark. I've tried to talk with you all these months, but you kicked and screamed so loudly you couldn't hear Me. It's okay. I know you're hurt. I've just had to hold you tightly until you could calm down. If you'll let Me now, I'll cradle you in My arms, and you can rest. You can trust Me. I won't let you go."

Emotionally, I felt the fight drain out of me. For the first time in months, I no longer had the strength to struggle. If I were to survive any longer, it would have to be with God's strength, not my own.

I looked at little Mark asleep in my arms. Suddenly I knew that just as I loved Mark and wanted what was best for him, God loved me, too. If Mark could trust me to love and protect him, I could trust God even more for His love and protection.

Like a little child, I saw myself crawl into God's arms. I felt them tighten around me and pull me close. I was so weary. Now I could rest in His arms.

Several years after the death of Sonny and Greg, God brought Max Greer, a widower, into Becky's life. They have been married 12 years.

31

When Hard Times Hit

Marta Haley Fields

Growing up, my parents had a little "nest egg," a savings account for emergencies. When I was 11, my father's employer of 35 years suddenly went out of business. My parents cracked that egg wide open.

Because of their foresight, our family survived two years of unemployment with few discomforts.

I wish my husband and I had had the inkling to tuck something aside, but with today's cost of living, we found it impossible to save money. When my husband, Zane, injured his back in a work-related accident, we were not prepared for the turmoil that followed.

We waited five months before Workers' Compensation agreed to pay disability. By then our credit was ruined. Although I had returned to work full-time, I didn't earn enough to keep our car from being repossessed. Surgery failed to correct Zane's painful back, so months of financial instability stretched into years. Had it not been for the love and generosity of God's people, it's doubtful our marriage could have survived the ordeal.

We're still going through hard times, but we're stronger because of them. Sadly, however, we're not alone in facing the reality of financial difficulties. America's economy, the experts tell us, is in a state of flux. A long list of companies is slashing operating costs—and announcing another round of layoffs. With all the dramatic changes in Eastern Europe, the U.S. defense industry faces drastic cutbacks.

While some feel that it's up to the federal and state governments to provide a "safety net" for those laid off, the Bible makes it clear the church should care for its own (see Galatians 6:10). Unemployment benefits do provide some help, but they cannot provide the love and acceptance a family so desperately needs when its world turns upside down.

What can you do to help families in need? Here are a few suggestions from someone who's been there:

• **Be sensitive.** Don't judge, especially if you don't have all the facts. My husband looks healthy enough, but he lives in constant pain. He doesn't work because he *can't* work. That doesn't make him a poor provider or a bad husband.

• **Don't confuse unemployment with irresponsibility.** Being out of work is embarrassing, even if jobs in your field are few and far between. We had a friend going through a period of no work. He dreaded going to church because he felt he needed to convince everyone he had "really" tried to find a job that week.

• **Don't flaunt your blessings.** During the worst of our troubles, I sang with a vocal ensemble. For weeks I sat silently during breaks while other women gabbed about what they had bought at the mall, what furniture they had ordered, or what new restaurant had just opened.

My idea of a good sale was whole chicken fryers for 49 cents a pound. I'm sure they had no idea they were excluding me, but it still hurt.

We have friends who have been blessed with a new home, a big car, and a fancy boat. Instead of telling us about their good times, Larry and Carol made us a part of them. We loved being invited over for burgers in their backyard. Another time, they invited us to the lake to fish and water-ski behind their new boat. Those were the only vacations we had for several years.

• **Pray for those going through tough times.** Ask the Lord how you can help. It can be as simple as going through your closet and passing along those clothes you rarely wear. Folks who can't afford new clothes attach no shame to hand-me-downs.

Our daughter's entire school wardrobe was provided by a co-worker's daughter who conveniently grew a size faster than Jessica each year.

• **Hard times place strains on a marriage that friends can help eliminate.** "Date nights" are the first thing to go when financial difficulties strike. Movie tickets are an extravagance, and the cost of a baby-sitter can do you in. Perhaps you can give gift certificates to the local movie theater or offer to watch the kids for an evening. A night away from the house can make a big difference to a marriage that's hurting.

• **Eating out is another luxury that's missed when the cash flow dwindles.** If you can afford it, ask a family out for lunch or dinner. From the outset, let them know it's your treat. Once we joined friends for lunch, but we ordered dinner salads (that's all we could afford) while they enjoyed a complete meal. Then they picked up the tab when the check arrived.

• **Remembering birthdays and anniversaries is a good way to meet emotional needs.** Socks and T-shirts were the gifts Zane and I exchanged on gift-giving occasions. But flowers or a thoughtful gift from a friend can provide moral support to a family that has given up everything but the essentials.

• **Helping out isn't restricted to just financial aid.** For someone who's sick or injured, a gift of your time can be the most valuable gift of all. Our yard suffered greatly after Zane's accident. Our friend Tom has come over several times to mow our lawn and trim the bushes.

• **Occasionally, a need becomes so pressing that it's no longer a case of simply giving up luxuries.** Necessities such as food and rent money are beyond the reach of many families. For months, we received groceries from a local food bank. Our church, which was aware of our need, actively supported the food bank. Some members of our congregation gave us gift certificates to local supermarkets, while others appeared on our doorstep with bags of groceries. What angels!

Should you ever loan money? Probably not. Loaning money can

drive a wedge between friends in a way that little else can. Even if you don't worry about being repaid, the person in debt does! Each time he sees you, all he sees is a big, fat IOU. And ultimately, you don't help a person in financial trouble by increasing his debt.

If you can afford to loan money for an extended period of time, you can probably afford to give it outright. Just be sure the need is real. When my car blew up, my church gave me $500 toward a new one. The elders knew that without transportation, I couldn't continue to work. We had many other pressing financial burdens, but this was one that could make or break us.

• **In extreme cases, it may become necessary to open up your home to someone in need.** Do so, but for the sake of your friendship, put limits on your hospitality. Whether it's three days or three months, make sure you set a time limit on their stay. Let them know your schedule and your housekeeping rules.

With the ground rules in place, realize that you may have to help them raise the first and last month's rent and security deposit required for rental units.

• **Finally, count your blessings.** No family is immune from hard times. Your job may look secure now, but that may not always be the case. All the money in the world won't eliminate the pain and confusion unemployment can bring to a family. Only God can bring the peace that passes all comprehension. It's to Him we must turn, in good times and bad.

Marta Field lives in Newbury Park, California.

32

Comeback

Dave Dravecky

C ancer came into my life as a small thing. I first noticed the lump in the fall of 1987.

When exactly, I do not even know. Running my hand along my left arm, it felt about the size of a quarter. It didn't hurt. It didn't show. And I paid little attention. That lump, which was to create so much turmoil in my life, made almost no impression on me at all.

As a matter of fact, my arm felt the best it had in years. During many of my six seasons with the San Diego Padres, my elbow had been sore. Since coming back to the San Francisco Giants, my arm had recovered. I was nearly pain-free. I felt on top of my game.

But in the 1988 season, I developed a sore shoulder. I'd typically start warming up, feeling fine. After three or four pitches, I would try to increase my velocity. That's when I would feel a small pop, as though I'd slightly dislocated my shoulder. Immediately, the pain was severe. I couldn't work through it at all, as I'd always been able to do before. I could hardly throw the ball.

The Giants' doctor, Gordon Campbell, examined me and recommended exploratory arthoscopic surgery. Ten days later, he was punching holes in me.

Peering into my inner workings, Dr. Campbell found a frayed tendon where the tip of the bicep muscle attaches to the shoulder. Apparently the frayed part was flopping and sticking in my shoulder joint when I flexed, and that was causing severe pain. Inserting a Roto-Rooter device, Dr. Campbell went in and shaved the frayed tendon. He cleaned out the scar tissue. Then he closed me up.

I began rehab. Atlee Hammaker, another Giants pitcher, and I hung around a lot together. Atlee was on me about the lump. "Man, that lump is getting bigger than your arm!" he'd say. I wasn't thinking about it. I was much more concerned about my shoulder.

Despite the operation, and despite all my hard work, my shoulder didn't seem to be getting any better. I was throwing the ball, but it still hurt. The 1988 season was a total loss for me. Before leaving the team, I talked with Dr. Campbell about getting an MRI (Magnetic Resonance Image) done on my lump. By then, the lump was clearly visible. It stood out on the side of my left arm like half a golf ball, and it was nearly as hard as one, too.

I had the MRI done on September 9, and the next day I went home to the family in Ohio. A few days later, I got a call from Dr. Campbell.

He talked in a gentle, businesslike voice. "Dave, there's a soft tissue mass on the end of your deltoid muscle," he said. "I've had some specialists look at the film, and they aren't sure what it is. It could be nothing, but I'd recommend you go see a doctor in your area." He knew a Dr. Bergfeld there, the team doctor for the Cleveland Indians. He said he'd get me an appointment.

In the Examining Room

The next day found my wife, Janice, and me in a little medical examining room at the Cleveland Clinic, waiting to be seen. A parade of medical people preceded Dr. Bergfeld.

One doctor asked me a lot of questions, took down my medical history, and inquired about other injuries, how long I'd played baseball, and so on. When he was gone, another group came in. They had me take my shirt off. They looked at my arm, felt it, rotated it.

We began to wonder whether we would ever see Dr. Bergfeld. Janice and I were talking quietly together when we heard the cadre of doctors shuffling around outside the door. Apparently, Dr. Bergfeld had arrived. The film from the MRI had been sent out from California. In low tones, the doctors were discussing what they saw. Then we heard the distinct words from one deep voice rising over the others.

"Look at that tumor."

Until that moment, no such possibility had crossed my mind, or Janice's either. I had thought we were there to have some scar tissue checked. We were just making sure everything was okay, just being careful.

When we heard the word *tumor*, it was as though the entire floor fell away and left us standing on a tiny chunk of safe ground hundreds of feet above a deep crevasse. Life, which had seemed so safe and pre- dictable only moments before, was now revealed to be on the verge of calamity.

I looked at Janice. She looked at me. I could see from her eyes that she was shocked and scared. But she's a strong person, and she initiated the right response. "I think we'd better pray," she said.

"Yeah," I said. "We'd better pray right now."

I got off the examining table and sat on a chair beside her. We held hands. It wasn't a long prayer.

"Dear God," I said, "we don't know what's happening. We don't know what this means. Help us to get through it, no matter what is involved. Help us to face whatever comes."

We ended quickly, because Dr. Bergfeld was coming in.

Hoping for the Best

Dr. Bergfeld took my arm, moved it around, examined it. He asked a few questions, then said, "Dave, this might be a tumor. We definitely need to do a biopsy on this. I'm going to send you up to see an oncologist."

When he said "oncologist," my heart skipped a beat. I know that an oncologist is a cancer doctor.

He kept talking calmly, though, as if we were discussing the weather.

"David, I don't think this is a malignant tumor. You've had it for over a year now, and the rate of growth is much slower than we would normally expect for a malignancy. But we need to be sure of that. So I want to send you up to see Dr. Muschler."

Dr. Bergfeld escorted Janice and me to the fifth floor to meet Dr. Muschler.

We shook hands in the hallway. I thought, *Man, this guy's hot off the presses.* He had wire-rim glasses and looked young enough to be taking his first college biology class. This was the doctor?

For what seemed to be the 30th time that day, my arm got examined. Dr. Muschler explored the flesh beneath the skin, moving my arm into various positions, touching that golf-ball-sized lump. Finally, he looked at me and said, "I recommend you have a biopsy on this. I don't think"—here he sounded just like Dr. Bergfeld—"I don't think we're dealing with a malignant tumor. But we can't be sure."

I wanted to jump out of my skin and say, "What do you mean you can't be sure? You're talking about my life!"

Janice responded in her typical responsible way. While I went off into deep space, she asked questions. She was astonished that Dr. Muschler could discuss a tumor so calmly—as though it were an ordinary event. Of course, in his medical profession, it is.

I asked when he wanted to do the biopsy. "As soon as possible," he replied.

Roots of Faith

I realize many people switch off when an athlete starts talking about God. They feel such talk cheapens the very personal issue of faith.

To some extent, I share that reaction. Some athletes use God like a trinket. They think if they latch on to God, they're going to go four-for-four, or they're going to hit a home run in the bottom of the ninth inning and win the ball game. Consequently, they show up for chapel services before a Sunday ball game. They think, *If I'm there and God sees me, He might honor my game today.*

That is bogus religion. It really shows a gigantic disrespect for God. Any genuine God of the universe must be a lot bigger than my desire to increase my batting average. If that's all God is to somebody, then God is just a superstition.

Maybe I feel so strongly about this because it's not too far from the image of God I once had.

I already knew there was a God. I considered myself a Christian, and I believed the Bible was God's Word. I got all that in my upbringing. But I had never read the Bible. Once, when we were first married, Janice suggested we read it together. Something in her church upbringing had given her the idea it would be a good thing for a married couple to do. But I had said no way. "I can't even read that thing, Janice. It doesn't make sense. If you want to read it, that's your business, but don't ask me to do it with you."

During the 1981 season, I was playing with the Amarillo team in Texas. One of the players I met was Byron Ballard. He had brilliant red hair and freckles; he was tall, with size 15 feet. I liked the guy immediately. Everyone did. He had a wonderful, zany sense of humor.

I saw some literature lying on his bed—Christian literature associated with baseball chapel. I commented on it, and during the next weeks, we talked again and again and again. Byron was not a guy to ram questions down my throat. On the contrary, I was asking questions.

Janice grew excited with me. We could see that if God was as personal as Byron—and the Bible—said, our basic orientation would have to change. If God truly cared about every detail of life, we couldn't any longer assume we knew what was best for ourselves, adding on God as an afterthought.

Eventually, we made a decision. We committed ourselves together to follow the personal God we learned about in the Bible, to follow Jesus wherever He might lead us.

God is personal. That lesson, learned in Amarillo, changed our lives forever. It transformed our response to the news we heard seven years later at the Cleveland Clinic following the biopsy operation.

Biopsy Results

"The biopsy shows it's just what we expected," said Dr. Muschler. "It's a fibrous tumor called a desmoid tumor." He explained that a desmoid tumor is not life threatening. But it was a threat to my arm. Of all cancerous tumors, the desmoid was probably the most likely to come back after an operation.

"If we leave one single cell in there, it can grow into another tumor, Dave. We have to cut it out with a wide margin all around. I'm afraid that means we'll have to take out at least half of your deltoid muscle."

Finally, when we talked through every medical angle I could think of, I asked him the question I knew was on everybody's mind—especially mine.

"What about my career?" I said. I could tell he had been dancing around the subject. "Tell it to me straight, Doc. I'm not afraid."

Dr. Muschler thought for a moment and then spoke quietly. "Well, Dave, if you have this operation, I think your chances of returning to professional baseball are zero. Losing half your deltoid muscle will take away one of the three most powerful muscles in your arm. My greatest hope is that after intensive therapy, you will regain a normal range of motion and be able to play catch with your son in the backyard."

The room was very quiet.

"You mean, no professional ball at all," I said.

He said no.

There was no hesitation in my mind. "Hey, Doc, if that's the way it is, let's get on with it. Don't think I'm going to go off in a little closet and cry. I've had a great career, I've enjoyed every minute of it, and I'm ready to go on with whatever is next."

That's what I said and what I truly felt. I told Dr. Muschler I'd been in an All-Star game. I'd pitched in two National League Championship Series and one World Series. I'd had a taste of every good thing baseball had to offer. What did I have to cry about?

"If I never play again, Doc, I'll know that God has someplace else. I believe in a God who can do miracles. If you remove half my deltoid muscle, that doesn't mean I'll never pitch again. If God wants me to pitch, it doesn't matter whether you remove all of the deltoid muscle. If God wants me to pitch, I'll be out there."

On October 7, 1988, surgeons removed one-half of the deltoid muscle in Dravecky's pitching arm. To kill all the cancerous cells, part of the humerus bone was frozen.

In January, doctors gave the okay to start a rehabilitation schedule. Dravecky made tremendous progress, and on August 10, 1989, he completed his comeback to the major leagues by taking the mound at Candlestick Park. He pitched eight strong innings against the Cincinnati Reds and earned the victory, 4-3. His incredible comeback captured the imagination of the country.

Less than a week later, however, Dravecky snapped the humerus bone in a game against the Montreal Expos. The bone was broken a second time during the victory celebration at the National League Championship Series.

On October 27, doctors at the Cleveland Clinic told Dravecky that cancer had probably recurred in his arm. Two weeks later, he announced his retirement from baseball. In January, doctors removed the second tumor and the remaining deltoid muscle in his arm.

Was the comeback worth it? Some people have asked whether it was worth struggling for that whole year in order to pitch only twice at the major league level. Was it worth it, considering how it ended in pain?

I don't even have to hesitate. Yes, it was worth it, a million times over. It was an unparalleled thrill. I got to live out the greatest boyhood dream of all. I got to do what the experts said was impossible, to come back from cancer and pitch a major league game. Without a deltoid muscle in my pitching arm, I won a game in a pennant drive in front of tens of thousand of screaming fans. What more would anybody want out of baseball?

It was worth it on another level, too. It was worth it because of the growth it brought in my life. I've learned a lot in the past two years. I've learned how precious my wife and my children are.

Such are the lessons that come when a man faces adversity. I don't think I could have gained them in any other way.

I'm clearly not done with adversity. My future is as unknown as before. All I can say for certain is that I'm done playing baseball.

There is no guarantee that I will get well, that I will overcome cancer, even that I will live another ten minutes. But Jesus Christ, the Son of God, was crucified and three days later rose from the dead, conquering death forevermore. As the Bible teaches in John 3:16, anyone who believes in Jesus will not perish but have everlasting life. He is the ground of my peace. With Him, I can face any adversity.

Dave Dravecky did, indeed, face more adversity, and in 1991, doctors amputated his left arm, plus part of his shoulder. He now travels around the country speaking to audiences about his experiences.

❧ PART FIVE ❧

FOCUS ON FAMILY HUMOR

33

God Can
Even Use
Cracked Pots

Patsy Clairmont

"Mommy, Mommy, Mommy, Mommy, Mommy, Mommy."
Marty's persistence matched his rhythmic tugging on
my blouse's hem.

I felt like screaming. In fact, I did.

To a little guy, my response was probably similar to the release of
Mount St. Helens as I erupted, "What?!"

Why a mother waits so long to respond and allows the repetition
to light her lava is beyond me. I only know that after spewing all over
him I felt terrible . . . and so did he. Where did all this volcanic anger
come from? I seemed to always be upset at something or someone.
Often my reactions were greater than the situation called for. I realized
that Marty's little-child ways didn't deserve such strong responses.

Have you ever tried making things right when you know you're wrong, but you don't know how to admit it or quit it? That was often my frustration with Marty.

I'd send him to his room, leaving me with the realization that his punishment was greater than his crime. Then I'd try to make up by slipping him a Twinkie or playing a game with him. I soon found that Twinkies don't build good bridges of communication—too squishy.

During a prayer time, as I cried out to the Lord for help with my temper, especially with my son, an idea formed that I believe was heaven-sent, because it made a difference.

I was to pray with Marty before I administered any form of discipline. Sometimes those prayers sounded strange and strained as I almost shouted, "Dear Lord, help this miserable little boy, and help his miserable mommy who wants so desperately to raise him in a way that would honor You."

By the time I said "amen," I was almost a reasonable person. I was able to see past my emotions and do what was in Marty's best interest.

Sometimes he needed a firm hand, but he was dealt with in love instead of anger, and the moment drew us together instead of tearing us apart. Many times, all he needed was time and a mother's tender touch.

But one day that boy really ticked me off! I remember heading across the room for him like a high-speed locomotive, steam coming out all sides. I had one goal and intent—get the kid, get the kid, get the kid!

Just as I loomed over him, his eyes the size of saucers, he held up one hand and yelled, "Let's pray!"

Marty had learned a valuable lesson in life. "When Mommy talks to Jesus, we're all a lot better off."

Who lights your lava?

Pricey

I have always wanted to play an instrument. Well, not any instrument. Mostly I dreamed of playing a piano. I pictured myself moving my fingers across the ivories without looking as I threw back my head and sang with throaty gusto. It didn't take me long to find out I couldn't sing. But piano . . . that took a little longer.

I was in my thirties when my friend Rose grew tired of hearing me whine about being deprived of piano lessons. She announced she would teach me. I was thrilled.

My husband lovingly, although somewhat reluctantly, moved an old upright into our living room. Those things weigh a ton. I could tell by the purple arteries that had inched their way out on his neck.

Not wanting his effort to be in vain, I began my serious study of the piano, certain I would soon be in concert. But I ran into an immediate problem. It was my teacher. She quite honestly was . . . boring. This surprised me, because Rose has a lot of verve. She usually was full of fun, but not so as a piano instructor.

She kept insisting I do scale exercises. Either of those words I avoid regularly; combined, they were depressing. Dull, repetitious pinging sounded childish.

I explained to her that this was not what I had in mind, so she agreed to teach me some real songs.

Now, when she said "real," I didn't know she was talking about "Old McDonald Had a Farm."

How do you think it looks and sounds to have a woman in her thirties e-i-e-i-o-ing? After a few weeks of musical farming, I'd had it, and so had my family. I could tell they were stressed when the veins on their temples seemed to pulsate in time to my barnyard plunking.

"I don't want to play 'Old McDonald.' I want to play 'How Great Thou Art,' " I stated with artistic fervor to Rose.

"You cannot play 'How Great Thou Art' until you first learn to play 'Old McDonald,' " Rose replied through tight teeth.

"How boring; how unimaginative," I complained.

"Patsy, you don't want to learn how to play the piano. You just want to play the piano," she accused.

Boy, did she hit a chord. No way was I willing to put in the time and effort necessary to become a pianist.

I gave up my musical illusions. Les and the boys joyfully, gratefully, and quickly removed the piano. Rose once again became her entertaining self.

What price is your dream?

Perks

Eve . . . what a perk-y lady! She definitely had advantages.

Stop and think about it. When she and Adam met, she didn't have to wonder, *Is this the right man for me?* She didn't have any immediate concerns if some sweet, young thing was vying for her man's attention.

When they were wed, she didn't have to worry about forgetting someone from the invitation list or deciding who the attendants would be. No decisions were necessary on which photographer, caterer, or florist to use. Talk about simplifying life . . .

Guess what? No mother-in-law or father-in-law conflicts. Never once did she have to hear, "Sure wish you could make applesauce like my mom." They never squabbled over whose family they would spend the holidays with.

She never had to worry about ironing Adam's dress shirts or getting the crease straight in his suit pants. There was no friction about Adam not picking up his dirty clothes, at least not in their garden home. Nor did she have to take any ribbing about where she put Adam's lost snakeskin sandals.

Eve was unique. She's the only gal who didn't have to go through puberty, peer pressure, or pimples. She didn't go through the agony of handing her parents a bad report card or the knee-knocking experience of trying to explain why she was late getting home. She never once had to hear her parents say, "Why aren't you more like your sister Ethel?"

When she and Adam talked, it wasn't filled with endless tales of the good ol' days and the good ol' boys. Nor did she have to compete with the World Series or the six o'clock Eden news report.

They had a romance, marriage, honeymoon, and home life that was made in paradise.

Eve had it all . . . well, almost all.

Why is it we always seem to want what we don't have?

Real Estate

My mom was a mover and a shaker. She loved moving from one home to another, and it would always shake me up!

I think moving was a hobby for her. She'd buy a house, fix it up, and sell it. Then she would start all over again. It always meant a different school and establishing new friendships. I made friends easily enough, but I hated leaving the old ones.

I decided when I grew up I would live in one house for the rest of my life. Then I married Leslie "The Mover" Clairmont.

Somehow my mom's mobility genes had bypassed me and entered Les. I didn't even realize that was possible.

I had felt safe marrying a man who had lived in only two homes from birth until marriage. But I counted recently, and in 28 years we have moved 23 times.

At about house number 17, I decided I had moveaphobia, and I wasn't going to pack one more time.

I cried out, "Lord, it isn't fair! You know a woman gets a lot of her security and identity from where she lives."

I tried to validate my opinion with Scripture. If I could do that, I figured the next time Les made me move, I could send him on a guilt trip.

The problem was I couldn't find any Scripture that suggested we should depend on a place, position, possession, or even person (other than Jesus) for our security and identity. I had to rethink my house "hold" and learn not to hang on so tightly.

I did feel encouraged when I read, "I go to prepare a place for you."

Notice "place" is singular. I don't have to take my Samsonite or rent one more U-Haul, y'all. I get to live in one place forever and ever. Amen.

The thought crossed my mind that when the Lord builds my husband's place, He should add on a room for my mom. Then He could put their mansion on rollers, and they could move all through eternity.

When they rolled by, I could lean out of my immovable place and wave. That would be heaven for us all!

Our home here is meant to be a haven. Heaven comes later.

Atmospheric Pressure

I don't feel well when I have to say "I'm sorry." I get strong, flu-like symptoms. I become nauseated. My knees get weak, my hands shake, and I get facial ticks.

If I have to say "I'm sorry and I was wrong," it's much worse. Then, along with the jerky behavior, my vision blurs, and my speech patterns slur.

I have noticed, though, that once I've said what needs to be said, I make an amazing recovery.

One day, Les was feeling frustrated with our eldest son over a work situation and needed to release a flurry of words. He came into my home office and spewed his displeasure about Marty onto me. Once Les said how he felt, he was ready to move past his aggravation.

After he left, I began to process their conflict and decided I could make the whole thing better. I envisioned myself as a Goodwill Angel (not to be confused with the Goodyear Blimp).

I fluttered into Marty's room and announced what he needed to do and when he needed to do it. For some reason, Marty was not impressed with this angelic visitation.

In fact, he told me, "If Dad has a problem with me that's job-related, then he can talk to me."

Well, Marty might be 25 years old, but how dare he insinuate I was butting in! Setting aside my helping halo, in my loudest mother's voice I trumpeted my heated annoyance. I finally ended my tirade by stomping up the steps. Marty placed his exclamation point on our meeting by slamming out of the house.

I packed away my singed raiment and was still sizzling when I heard Les come in. I went down to make a pronouncement on his son's poor behavior. By the look on Les's face, it was obvious he had already encountered Marty.

"If I had wanted you to go to Marty, I would have asked you," he stated through clenched teeth. "Patsy, this was none of your business."

"None of my business!" I bellowed. A cloudburst of tears followed as I ran to my room, tripping several times on my lopsided wings.

"I was only trying to help," I kept consoling myself.

When the tears and excuses stopped, I began to wonder if maybe I could have been wrong. Flu-like symptoms intensified when I realized I needed to apologize to both of them for interfering.

By the time I made my way out to Les and Marty, my vision had blurred. My head was pounding (probably from that heavy halo) as I stammered the dreaded words, "I-I was wr-wrong for interfering. I'm sorry. Will you f-forgive me?"

Within moments we were all hugging.

As I walked back to the house, I noticed my headache and vexed vision had vanished, and it was almost . . . as if my feet weren't touching the ground.

Hey, Angel Face, anyone in your sphere deserve an apology?

Patsy Clairmont first became known to Focus on the Family's audience when she was Dr. Dobson's guest on the daily radio program in 1989. This article is excerpted from her book *God Uses Cracked Pots*. Published by Focus on the Family.

❧34

Childbirth 101

Philip Wiebe

*T*he birth last summer of our son, Seth, made me realize
parenting is a breeze compared to something so frightening, so
intimidating, so mind-numbing that it should have been an
episode of "The Twilight Zone."

What I'm talking about, of course, is the *anticipation* of parenthood.

I mean, after my wife, Kimberly, broke the Big News, I had questions. Are we going to have a boy or a girl? Will we use cloth or plastic
diapers? Are we going to use a bottle or, uh, a nonbottle?

Fortunately, our local hospital offered a refreshing resource to help
us prepare for the long days and longer nights of first-time parenthood.
But enough about their new gourmet coffee bar—what we needed was
a childbirth class. Good thing our local hospital offered one of those,
too. And I can truly say it helped us view the whole thing in a much
broader perspective. In other words, it made the anticipation *even
worse*. Here's a breakdown:

Week One—Nutrition. I was hoping for some audience participa-
tion, like maybe one involving deep-dish pepperoni pizza, but alas, it

was straight lecture. We covered such thrilling topics as: (1) the rewards of a proper diet; (2) the need for adequate exercise; and (3) the evils of deep-dish pepperoni pizza. Kimberly vowed (again) to wean me from the stuff, but I (as always) came up with a brilliant defense:

"Sorry, dear, but all this nutrition talk is for you. You're the one carrying the baby."

"Listen, buster. You need to live long enough to raise this baby, too. How does oat bran and a brisk walk in the morning sound to you?"

Not too good, I thought, but she did have a point.

Week Two—Labor and Delivery. We watched a video called "The Miracle of Birth." During the graphic parts, some fathers—heh, heh—actually looked away. Not me. You'd be surprised how much you can still see through the little cracks between your fingers.

From the parts my knuckles didn't block, I gathered that natural childbirth includes:

- heavy breathing
- fainting
- hyperventilation
- pain
- screaming

Oh, and I guessed it wouldn't be a bed of roses for Kimberly, either.

Week Three—Cesarean Delivery. Well, no problem here. Low-odds stuff never happens to us, especially when it involves winning magazine publishers' sweepstakes.

Besides, I skipped this lesson. I knew what thrilling slides lay in store for me. Once, my friend Joe stuck photos of his wife's cesarean in my face. I almost lost my lunch. If Kimberly ever had one, I knew I wouldn't be able to eat dinner for *years.*

Week Four—Caring for Newborns. We learned the absolute number-one thing we need to do to effectively include a new baby in our lifestyle—knock out the back of our house. How else were we going to find room for all the "essentials": cribs, cradles, swings, walkers, changing tables, mobiles, bottles, burp rags, baby wipes, nummies . . .

Nummies!

"Say," I inquired at the class, "what *are* those things, anyway?"

"Oh," the instructor replied, "it's another word for pacifiers. You know, those rubber plugs for quieting your little precious during fussy periods."

Patting Kimberly on the arm, I offered, "Like before she's had her morning Mueslix?"

Believe me, that would have been a great time to try one of those nummies out.

Week Five—Bottle Versus, Uh, Nonbottle Feeding. They filled us in on the specific advantages of each:

- Nonbottle is nature's way, plus you always have it with you.
- Bottle means you can delegate all those grueling, middle-of-the-night feedings to your husband.

I wanted to go with nonbottle, for sure. Hard to argue with nature. But Kimberly had other ideas.

Week Six—Father's Role. The times, they are a-changing. My father's role was to pace the waiting room and pass out chocolate cigars. Apparently my role was to pass out. Because, as a modern father, I got to:

- Be the labor and delivery "coach," which should be interesting for someone who gets queasy just walking into a hospital and taking a deep breath.
- Be responsible for the CDs. Yes, I got to take care of those little "certificates of deposit" our little one would leave behind.
- Do all those grueling, middle-of-the-night feedings. But I recently heard about this new thing called, uh, a nonbottle pump, and if I ever get my hands on the person who invented it . . .

Week Seven—Getting Through Labor. I made some unnecessary cracks about my already knowing all this by virtue of belonging to a labor union. Frankly, if I'd wanted 156 straight weekends of diaper duty, I would have asked for it. Come to think of it, maybe I did.

The last baby class wasn't the end of my education. Waiting for the Big Moment can teach you a lot. Such as:

1. Sleeping on a waterbed with a restless, nine-months-pregnant woman makes you wonder if you should have taken that Caribbean cruise in the first place.

2. Pleading "sympathy pregnancy" to justify a midnight pizza run never works.

3. When people said kids slow you down, I'd always thought that meant feeding, changing, napping, bonding, and so on. Now I realize they were talking about that hundred-pound diaper bag you have to lug around.

4. Distinguishing false labor from the Real Thing is hard, but not as hard as the ceiling you bash your head on every time your wife whispers "Phil!" in the middle of the night.

5. To the earnest folks who assured us the labor and delivery process isn't really that bad, we need to say from the bottom of our hearts, "You're wrong, people!" Fifteen hours of hard labor isn't a piece of cake, especially when the reward you finally hold in your hands is not a new baby, but the release form for a cesarean section.

A cesarean section! So it *could* happen to us. Faced with this sobering reality, it was time to count blessings. For instance, I'm grateful Joe forgot to bring any photos to stick in my face. I'm thankful the hospital staff was skilled and dedicated. And that family and friends were there for moral support. And, as it turned out, for a successful surgery, quick recovery, and the wonderful birth of a thriving baby boy. And even for nummies, which have helped smooth out those post-hospital fussy times. One of these days, we may even let Seth have one.

As predicted, however, I haven't been myself for a while. Because now you can call me "Dad." And if I'm never myself again, it's okay by me.

Philip Wiebe has purchased a dozen nummies for his young son, Seth, but he can never find one when he needs to. The Wiebes live in Salem, Oregon.

❧35

Why My Hubby Takes Lots of Pictures

Rosie B. Jones

I first realized my husband's condition on our honeymoon. We strolled past a specialty camera shop, and Daron gasped. His face grew red, his eyes bugged out, and he almost tripped over his own big feet.

I reached out my hand to support him in case he fell.

That's when I discovered the lump.

On his chest.

It was an Instamatic camera.

"I always carry one of these around my neck," he told me, "close to my heart."

Some husbands watch too much football. Some leave their clothes lying around. Others track mud over the floor. Mine takes pictures.

With a little effort, you can pick up clothes and wipe up mud.

Even football season ends. But the wife of a camera bug has no relief.

Sometimes it starts early in the morning when the birds chirp.

Tweet. Tweet. Serenity until—*click.*

"Aak! You got me sleeping! My hair's messed up! I haven't put any makeup on . . ."

"Honey, you don't need makeup. You look fine first thing in the morning." He pats his camera as he trots away. "Someday you'll be glad I took that picture!"

Dinnertime

When company comes, he pulls out all the picture boxes. "See," he says as he flails photos every which way, "this is Rosie eating spaghetti."

After a couple of years of my nagging, hiding the camera between Christmas and birthdays, and complaining about the price of film, I persuaded him to cut back to a roll a week.

Then I got pregnant.

I gave up hope of any restraint when he began having me pose everyday. Never mind my face—he delighted in taking pictures of my expanding tummy.

Soon the happy day arrived. Daron brought our secondhand super 8 movie camera to the birthing room.

"I'm not having this baby until you turn that thing off!" I insisted between contractions.

After our son, Stephen, was born, we had to adjust our budget. Baby things didn't cost so much—it was the price of film and developing that was out of sight.

I can hear father and son playing in the living room right now. "Let's see a smile, Stephen!"

Click.

"Dada."

"He said it! Did you hear that, Rosie? He said dada!"

Click. Click. Click.

This obsessive picture-taking was annoying, but my troubles tripled when I absentmindedly flipped through some mail coupons. "Say, Daron," I called to him one evening as he was giving Stephen a bath. "Look at this—a father/son photo contest. First prize is a camcorder."

Glue my mouth shut. I'd forgotten there's no higher prize for a camera bug than a camcorder. Daron almost dropped his 35mm Canon into the bathwater.

Immediately, he pulled Stephen out of the tub and draped a fluffy towel around him. Bouncing him on his knee, Daron handed me his camera.

"This shot will win the photo contest, Hon!"

Now *I* had to take pictures.

"But . . . I'm not a photographer," I complained.

"You just missed his smile!"

Click. "Okay, that's good enough."

"Wait! I can get him to smile real big."

Click. "How's that?"

"That wasn't *real* big. Just wait. Gitchy goo. Stephen . . ."

I already had eyestrain.

Waiting for the Right Shot

This went on for weeks. Every time I took a roll of snapshots, I threatened to sell the camera.

The day we had a big snow, Daron envisioned the "winning" picture.

"Stephen and I will wear our matching Mickey Mouse stocking caps," he said. "We'll pose in front of the snowman I just made."

I grumbled as we trudged outside in the snow. I put the camera to my eye.

"Now wait for the right shot," he instructed—as usual.

"I can take the picture without help from you," I balked. The sun had come out that day, and as I looked through the viewfinder, I could see the snowman sweating. Within minutes, dismembered snowman parts rolled across the lawn.

The timing was bad, but then again, maybe it wasn't. Now I didn't have to take any more snowman pictures.

Daron didn't smile. "I can't believe you missed that," he whined. "The snowman falling apart would have been a winning picture. There goes my camcorder."

"Well, how was I supposed to know you wanted a picture of the snowman falling apart?" I retorted. "I don't like taking pictures anyway."

"I guess we'll have to try again," Daron said as he began reassembling Mr. Snowman.

"No way," I cried. "I've got eyestrain, and all you do is boss me around. I'm never taking another picture for you. Here, take your old camera!"

"I'm sorry, Honey." Daron surely couldn't be as humble as he looked. "I never meant to boss. I'd just like to win a camcorder, because Stephen won't be little for very long. Anyway, these snapshots will be even more special to us 20 years from now."

I wanted to argue, but what he said reminded me of something. Perhaps it was the Holy Spirit's nudge—I don't know. When Daron and I dated, one of the things that drew me to him was his love of family.

When his mother made her first sale as a Realtor, he took her a rose. I knew then I would get roses, too.

And he changes diapers.

"I'm sorry for complaining," I mumbled.

"I forgive you, Hon."

He hugged my shoulder. "Now let's get this snowman ready for that winning picture."

Rosie Jones says Daron desperately wants a new telephoto lens for Christmas. The Joneses live in Vancouver, Washington.

36

Holding Down the Fort While Mom's Gone

Bob Welch

In the beginning were the words. They came from my seven-year-old son, Ryan, shattering my Saturday morning slumber with all the subtlety of a low-flying F-15. For parents of small children, they are the eight most feared words in the English language:

"Don't worry, Dad, I fixed my own breakfast."

Still in my pajamas, I dragged myself to the scene of the crime.

Indeed, my son had fixed his own breakfast—a bowl of Alphabits cereal (which explained why the kitchen floor was strewn with enough letters to spell the entire lineage of David). I sighed. This was going to be an interesting two weeks.

The previous night, my wife, Sally, had left on a short-term missionary trip. Her goal was to bring medicine, encouragement, and the gospel to the needy people of Haiti. Mine was less lofty: to have a measurable pulse when she returned. But now that it's over, I not only have a healthy pulse, but also a special message for my comrades.

We have it easy.

I'm not trying to rain on anybody's parade, but given that humility precedes honor (see Proverbs 15:33), let's humble ourselves, dads, by admitting we're spoiled rotten. We take the kid to a ball game; our wives get the grit.

It starts early, with the birth of the child. The woman has just spent nine months throwing up, gaining weight, craving peanut-butter enchiladas, and trying to get out of the car without accidentally honking the horn. Meanwhile, the man's challenge has been in trying to sneak a pillow into the natural childbirth classes.

But when the child is born, guess who's on the phone soaking up the congratulations ("piece o' cake," he tells his friends) while Mom recovers in a sitz bath?

A "Mr. Mom" Experience

The gap widens as Junior grows. We fathers sit in our offices, sneaking a peak at toothless baby pictures. Meanwhile, Mom is home, cutting Silly Putty out of the little tyke's hair while simultaneously lifting the refrigerator to retrieve an overdue library book. And if she's working outside the home, guess who winds up with those duties that evening—after dragging a young Duck-Duck-Goose player home from the child-care center?

If you dads want to unspoil yourselves, try being moms for a while. It's guaranteed to shrink your ego and enlarge your appreciation for the magic worked by your wife—and those single parents out there.

This insight comes after my minor-league "Mr. Mom" experience. While Sally was gone, I lived on Easy Street for much of the time. Friends from our church delivered hot meals most nights. Others watched the two boys—seven-year-old Ryan and four-year-old Jason—until I arrived home from work. But even with such support, I came away feeling as if I'd just been through the W-4 form of parental experiences.

As a single parent, the first thing I learned was that if you don't do something, it ain't gonna get done. And if by some small miracle it does get done, it ain't gonna get done right. Before Sally left, I just assumed that whenever you ran out of soap, the Soap Fairy magically replenished the dish. I also imagined that the Soap Fairy had relatives—the Milk Fairy, the Dental Floss Fairy, and the Light Bulb Fairy, among others. As Mr. Mom, I learned the only things in a household that magically replenish themselves are laundry, dirty dishes, and junk mail.

I now understand why God said it is not good for a man to be alone. He knew what we needed: a helpmate who knows instinctively how to remove strawberry Jell-O stains from a pet rabbit. One who also knows you can't make whipped cream out of Half 'n' Half and that certain antistatic thingamajigs go in the dryer along with the clothes. I learned that after noticing Jason was walking around with something clinging to the back of his sweatshirt—a pair of static-laden Batman undershorts.

I pressed three dress shirts before realizing the iron was not plugged in. I let so much toothpaste build up in the kids' sink that I could have chipped it off and had a week's supply of breath mints. On one short trip we took, I packed two right-footed boots—and no left—for my oldest son. And somehow, I wound up with nine widowed socks!

But socks weren't the only thing that got lost—so did my time with the kids—and my patience. I discovered that left unattended, house plants don't thrive. And neither do children, who need emotional watering to flourish. But who has the time when the house looks like Oscar Madison's bedroom?

A Transformation Hits

Too often, I'd plunk the kids in front of a Disney video so I could do more important things, like scraping last night's lasagna from the dining-room table or embarking on a search-and-destroy mission for moldy food in the fridge.

I got grumpy. I was transformed from Guy Smiley to Oscar the Grouch. Early on, I kept my cool. When Ryan locked half the neighborhood in a pup tent, I handled the episode without even raising my voice. But when he used a fork to catapult lima beans at his brother across the dinner table, I became John McEnroe after a bad call.

An uneasy truce ensued, but on day 12 (after forgetting to give Ryan his lunch money for the second day in a row), I sensed a smidgen of lost confidence in me. "I want Mom back," Ryan informed me.

"Me, too," Jason piped up.

It was time to play my trump card. The kids wanted to paint their wooden sailboats, so I obliged. I made sure the paint was water-soluble. After what I'd been through, the last thing I needed was a set of permanently stained shirts.

How was I to know that my sons were planning to launch their freshly painted boats in the bathtub? "Dad, all the paint washed off," said Jason, sitting in a tub of tomato juice.

I drained the Red Sea and thanked God that bedtime was finally here. While putting the kids to bed, the phone rang. Happily, I thought perhaps things in Haiti had gone so smoothly that my wife's missionary team was coming home a day early.

Not quite. But for a limited time only, I could have my drapes dry-cleaned for a special low, low price.

"Uh, thanks, but—"

The buzzer sounded from the basement. My washer was lopsided again.

"Dad, you forgot to go over my spelling words with me," Ryan yelled from his bunk.

That's when the pet rabbit knocked over the wooden Noah's Ark puzzle, scattering elephants, zebras, and giraffes across the living room, two by two.

In retrospect, though, I suppose it's good these things happened. Sometimes we men need to walk a mile in our wives' Reeboks to appreciate everything they do, discover everything we *don't* do, and realize how we can be better husbands and fathers.

So this year, when my wife and kids gather around to celebrate Father's Day, I'm going to have a new perspective. If we fathers stand proudly at the helm, it's our wives who keep the ship afloat.

Still, after my pinch-hitting experience, I remain mystified by two things: How do mothers do it—juggle family, home, and sometimes a job? And, perhaps even more mind-boggling, just where *are* those missing socks?

Bob Welch never did find those socks in his home in Eugene, Oregon.